sew your own
animal dolls

sew your own
animal dolls

25 **CREATIVE DOLLS TO MAKE AND GIVE**

Louise Kelly

CICO BOOKS

LONDON NEW YORK

Published in 2018 by CICO Books
An imprint of Ryland Peters & Small Ltd
20–21 Jockey's Fields   341 E 116th St
London WC1R 4BW   New York, NY 10029

www.rylandpeters.com

10 9 8 7 6 5 4 3 2 1

Text © Louise Kelly 2018
Design, illustration, and photography © CICO Books 2018

A CIP catalog record for this book is available from the Library of Congress and the British Library.

ISBN: 978-1-78249-642-7

Printed in China

Editor: Kate Haxell
Designer: Alison Fenton
Photographer: Geoff Dann
Illustrator: Cathy Brear
Template illustrations: Kate Haxell
Stylist: Nel Haynes

In-house editor: Anna Galkina
Art director: Sally Powell
Production manager: Gordana Simakovic
Publishing manager: Penny Craig
Publisher: Cindy Richards

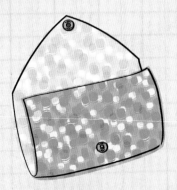

contents

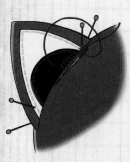

introduction

Mother Nature is truly a wonder, just think of how many majestic, strange, and cute creatures there are in the world—I had an unlimited source of inspiration for this book.

I have always been an animal lover, but while brainstorming and researching lots of different species and really looking closely at them, I fell in love all over again. If you aren't lucky enough to have a real one to gaze at, try to find a photo or a video of a red panda; notice its gorgeous markings, its deep lush color, how it moves, and the shape of its ears. Or perhaps have a look at a fennec fox, which is so breathtakingly beautiful it's hard to believe it's even real! The world is full of amazing creatures, how could I possibly choose which ones to make into dolls?

I began by sketching—as I usually do—all the animal characters I could envisage, wondering what they would be wearing, or where they would be going, what would their names be? If I was a koala going to lunch with the girls, what would I put on? I invariably love the whole of the doll-making process, every step of it brings me such joy, but this part—the sketching and inception of my little characters—is so exciting and invigorating that I can hardly sleep for thinking about color and fabric and stitches.

I do so hope that you feel the same way once you flip through this book. How wonderful it would be for this book to spark your imagination and creativity, for you to feel so excited by what you find within its pages that you can hardly wait to get started.

So, go now and have a look: choose your favorite animal and build its very own outfit from all the patterns in the clothing and accessories section, then get to snipping and stitching. And once you are done and your little critter has a name, come find me on social media at @ loulovesthis and show me what you've made—I would love to see!

Happy doll-making,

Louise

materials & tools

It is essential to choose good-quality materials—not only will they give you a great finished doll, but they are also a pleasure to work with. You don't need many tools and most are inexpensive, but it's also a good idea to buy the best quality you can afford. Sewing is a very tactile occupation, so lovely fabrics and textures make it really worthwhile and enjoyable.

Each project gives fabric quantities that will be sufficient if you arrange the template and pattern pieces carefully.

felt

Good-quality felt is one of the most important elements in creating a doll. It doesn't have to be expensive; there are many beautiful felts out there for great prices. Choose a felt that is either made from 100 percent wool, or a wool mix felt that has at least 30 percent wool. Pure wool felt used to be very coarse and thick, but these days you can find sturdy yet smooth, soft, and fine wool felt in a vast array of colors. Avoid 100 percent acrylic felt; it won't hold up to a lot of stitching, can become misshapen when stuffed, you can't iron it (it will melt), and it can have a squeaky feel when working with it. It can also pill or get bobbly, and it certainly won't help create a long-lasting doll.

stuffing

Polyester toy stuffing is widely available, from craft stores and online; buy a big bag and it will last for ages.

thread

I mainly use six-stranded embroidery floss (thread) and almost always use just one strand of it, so I cut a length and separate off one strand each time I need a length of thread. You could also use a spool of cotton or polyester sewing thread, which I sometime use for neutrals or colors that I tend to use a lot of. Whichever you choose, one thin strand and a fine needle will be delicate enough for sewing small pieces of felt and cotton.

Embroidery floss (thread) is fairly inexpensive, so it's a great way of building a thread collection if you need a lot of different colors, but it is always best to choose a good-quality brand; I know from experience that cheap floss (thread) is terrible to work with, as it tangles and breaks easily (see the suppliers on page 135 for my favorite brands). I think of my thread collection as a painter's palette: I keep it in a thread organizer box, each shade wound onto a little card bobbin, and grouped into color families so that I can clearly see all the shades at a glance—and what I need to replenish.

cotton fabric

I prefer to use good-quality cotton fabric to make the dolls' clothes—especially pretty vintage prints. I source most of my fabrics from patchwork and quilting stores or online suppliers, where you can buy individual fat quarters (one yard (meter) of fabric cut into four pieces) in a wide range of prints and colors. You can easily get three or four dresses from one fat quarter. Old clothes, such as dresses with a pretty pattern or shirts and t-shirts, can also be recycled.

building your stash

You may already have a collection of fabrics, ready to get started making outfits for your dolls. If you don't have a stash, here are a few tips on how to build one. All you need are a few feature prints that really speak to you, a few polka dots and stripes that match, some neutrals and animal-colored felts, a few felt colors for shoes and hair flowers, maybe a fat quarter of denim, and instantly, you have a potential capsule wardrobe ready to sew for your doll!

• Begin by picking the colors and patterns that you like, these will be your feature fabrics. This may seem obvious, but you are the person who will be using them so they should make your heart sing! Don't like florals? Then choose some geometrics or novelty prints. Don't like bright pastel color schemes? Then go for autumnal or primary colors. My feature fabrics are usually florals and often Liberty of London prints—they produce such wonderful tiny florals.

• Once you have your feature fabrics you need to source your "basics." For me these are polka-dot and striped fabrics and, of course, solid-color cottons; I like to keep a good stock of these in a variety of colors. I use them for doll underwear, a blouse to match a flowery skirt, or a contrasting bodice in a dress. Keep your feature fabrics in mind when buying your basics, so that you can mix and match fabrics that complement each other.

• Also keep your eye out for other, more unusual, fabrics to add to your stash: soft cotton-mix denims, lace, tulle, jersey knit, faux suede, and glitter fabrics.

basic sewing kit

You don't need many tools to start sewing your own dolls. These are the essential items you should have to hand in your sewing kit.

needles

The wrong needle can ruin your project and the right one will make sewing a breeze. I favor fine needles and almost exclusively use size 10 sharps. For me, they are perfect for sewing small things. If you use a needle that is too big or thick, it could disrupt or tear the edge of your felt, and the seams won't hold up to stuffing. You will also need a doll needle, which is very long, for attaching limbs.

glue pen

My fabric glue pen is the most favored and trusted tool in my kit! Although I do use pins or basting (tacking) to hold larger pieces in place for sewing, often the pattern pieces are too small to take a pin. This is where the glue pen comes in; I use it to secure small hems and seam allowances, keep eyes and noses in place while they are being stitched, and for a multitude of other little bits and pieces. The glue dries clear (except on very dark fabrics, where it will dry white-ish), it's very easy to sew through, and it doesn't gum up your needle. It's also washable and non-permanent. I use a Sewline fabric glue pen, as they can be refilled easily.

pins

For the same reasons that I choose fine needles, I always use fine pins—they slip through the fabric and felt without tearing or leaving puncture marks.

fabric pens, markers, and pencils

I have tried many different fabric-marking tools over the years; some can be removed with water while some are air-erasable, and you can even use felt tips, rollerballs, pencils, or discs of chalk. Some markers even come with their own erasing fluid! But by far my most favored fabric-marking tools are the ones with thermo-sensitive inks (in other words, heat-erasable): the ink in these pens becomes transparent with friction or heat. I use them for drawing around templates, adding seam allowances, and sketching features directly onto felt, and I use a hairdryer to remove the marks when I'm finished. In my experience the marks always disappear easily this way, but you should test it on a scrap of fabric if you are concerned.

Making marks on dark fabrics requires a different tool—I love the Sewline Fabric Pencil, which works just like a regular mechanical pencil, except that it uses ingenious ceramic leads (I especially like the white or pink leads). You can get far more accurate marks with it than with tailor's chalk or a fabric chalk pencil.

hemostats (haemostats)

This little tool changed my dollmaking! Hemostats help you to push the stuffing into the nooks and crannies of the sewn-up pieces without having to squish or crumple your fabric, which is especially useful for limbs and heads. They allow you to vary the firmness of the stuffing, too. They are also incredibly useful when it comes to turning bodies, limbs, and heads the right way out after stitching. Essentially hemostats look like a long pair of tongs and you can buy them for crafting from most good stores in a range of sizes; I recommend the 6in (15cm) or 8in (20cm) ones. The alternative is to use the end of a pencil to push stuffing into limbs, although you won't get as much control.

scissors

Who doesn't love a beautiful pair of scissors? Here are the types you need to see you through all your dollmaking projects:

• A small pair of embroidery scissors—perfect for snipping threads and cutting small pattern pieces.

• A larger pair of fabric shears—for cutting larger pattern pieces and general fabric use.

• A pair of pinking shears, which are great for cutting cotton or other fabric that may fray, and for creating decorative edges.

Scissors can range in price from cheap to astronomical but, as with most crafting tools, it's a good idea to invest in a really good pair of fabric scissors; if you look after them well, they will last you a lifetime. Never EVER let anyone use your fabric scissors for cutting paper or wire or anything other than fabric and thread!

other miscellaneous items

I always have a small 6in (15cm) quilter's ruler within arm's reach when I'm working—I use it to add seam allowances and check measurements, because it gives really accurate results.

I also find tear-away stabilizer useful when embroidering eyelashes, as it adds structure to the fabric and really holds the stitches in place. When you're done, you just tear away the excess.

And last, but not least, some cardstock for cutting out templates, and a pair of papercutting scissors—don't ever use your fabric scissors!

techniques

If you have previously done any sewing then you will already be familiar with most of the techniques used in this book. It's always a good idea to try out anything new to you on a scrap of fabric or felt before starting your project.

using templates

Templates for all the pattern pieces used in this book are given on pages 122–134; they are printed at 50 percent of their actual size, and will need to be enlarged by 200 percent using a photocopier before you use them.

Many of the dolls are made in the same way, so you'll use the same templates for the basic doll over and again (depending on how passionate about dollmaking you become!). Similarly, the garment patterns are used for multiple dolls, so these will also be used many times. You can photocopy the templates as you need them (no need to do them all at once), cut them out, and use these paper shapes to draw around onto your felt or fabric. However, if you draw around or trace them onto card, then cut them out, you will have sturdy, reusable templates; this is what I do and I find it very useful. I keep my templates in a little expandable file, with compartments for body and limbs, heads, ears and noses, clothes, shoes, and accessories so that I can always find what I need.

Some of the templates include stitching lines and seam allowance guides, so refer back to the template section where necessary.

handstitching doll bodies

All the dolls in this book are handstitched, which is my favorite way to work. If you have never handstitched before, or haven't done much of it, I would really encourage you to try—it has such a lovely gentle rhythm. However, if you are adept and confident with your sewing machine, then you could machine-sew some of the steps.

I use a small backstitch—working just a fraction of an inch (few millimeters) in from the edge of the fabric—to put the bodies together. Small, regular stitches are ideal, but don't worry about making them absolutely perfect, as the most important thing is to create nice clean lines and strong seams that will withstand firm stuffing. Backstitch is especially helpful for making curved seams.

To start sewing, knot the end of the thread as you normally would, but instead of tying a knot when you finish that length of thread, or line of stitching—which can be cumbersome—just weave the needle and thread through the back of a few stitches and snip off the excess thread. At each turning gap, make a few stitches on top of each other to really strengthen the end of the seam.

hand stitches

The stitches used to sew the dolls and to create their faces are not difficult to work, but if you are new to embroidery then I advise you to practice the stitches using the correct fabrics and thread before you start work on your doll's face.

running stitch

This is a basic stitch that has many applications. It creates a broken or dashed line, and is both functional and decorative. Basting (tacking) stitch involves making longer running stitches to temporarily hold layers of fabric together while they are sewn with a smaller, more regular stitch—the basting (tacking) stitches are then removed.

Simply bring the needle up and back down through the fabric, keeping the spaces between the stitches the same length as the stitches themselves.

whip stitch

This is a decorative and functional overcast stitch. It is a very quick way of attaching one layer of fabric to another, or seaming the edges of two or more layers of fabric. In this book it is mostly used for attaching noses, muzzles, and inner ears, and for making doll shoes.

To seam two pieces, from the wrong side push the needle up through one layer of fabric. Take the needle over the edge of both pieces, then bring the needle back through both layers of fabric so it comes out of the same hole, making an initial, straight, anchoring stitch. Take the needle over both edges again and through the layers so that it comes out a short distance from the first stitch. Continue in this way to make a series of sloping, parallel stitches.

To attach one layer to another, from the wrong side push the needle up through both layers of fabric. Then take the needle over the edge of the smaller piece and down through the larger piece. Bring the needle up through both layers of fabric, so that it comes out a short distance from the first stitch. Continue in this way to make a series of sloping, parallel stitches.

backstitch

The most widely used stitch throughout the book, backstitch is both decorative and functional. It creates a continuous line of stitches, which is perfect for seams and hems, and also for adding detail to faces and around eyes.

Bring the needle up from the back, one stitch length to the left of your start point. Insert it one stitch length to the right (so, at the start point), and then bring it up again one stitch length in front of the point where the needle first emerged. Always work back into where the last stitch ended to make an unbroken line.

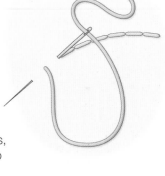

blanket stitch

This stitch is both decorative and functional and is often used in appliqué and for sealing the edges of fabric. Throughout this book it is used to attach eyes, noses, and other features, and along the edges of felt garments.

From the wrong side, bring the needle through close to the edge of the fabric. From the right side, push the needle back through the fabric a short distance from the edge and loop the thread under the needle. Pull the thread through to make the first stitch. Push the needle back through the fabric a short distance to the right and loop the thread under the needle to make a second stitch. Continue in this way.

satin stitch

Satin stitch is a decorative filler stitch. It is a wonderful stitch to learn and is used for some pretty decorative floral embroidery on Abbi's dress (see page 36).

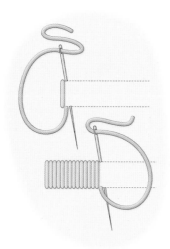

Make a series of straight stitches laid close together to completely fill a shape without any gaps.

ladder stitch

Ladder stitch is a functional and very handy stitch to know. It is used to seamlessly close the turning gaps on doll bodies and limbs after stuffing, and to attach ears—and tiny elephant trunks. It can also be used to repair a tear or an uneven seam.

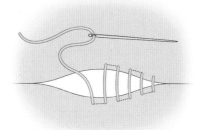

Catch the first edge with your needle and make a very small stitch. Cross to the other side of the seam (or work from head to ear), and make up a tiny stitch a short distance away from the edge, then return to the other side, again picking up a short distance away from the edge. Work a few stitches before pulling them closed, and then continue along the gap.

lazy daisy

A pretty, decorative stitch that can be used to make single loops, or several can be grouped to make a flower.

From the wrong side, push the needle up through the fabric. Take it back through very close to where it came out and make a short stitch. Before pulling the needle through the fabric, wrap the working thread under the tip of the needle, then pull the needle and thread through to make the first stitch. Take the needle back down very close to where it last came out and repeat to make a second stitch. Continue in this way.

french knot

A purely decorative stitch and very versatile, a knot is created on the surface of your work by wrapping the thread around the needle. Various sizes can be achieved by using different threads and more or fewer wraps. I use them for highlights in the doll's eyes.

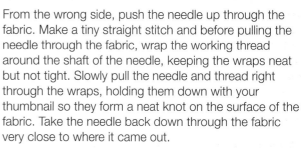

From the wrong side, push the needle up through the fabric. Make a tiny straight stitch and before pulling the needle through the fabric, wrap the working thread around the shaft of the needle, keeping the wraps neat but not tight. Slowly pull the needle and thread right through the wraps, holding them down with your thumbnail so they form a neat knot on the surface of the fabric. Take the needle back down through the fabric very close to where it came out.

embroidering eyes

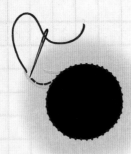

1 Glue the felt eye in position and either blanket stitch (see page 11) or whip stitch (see page 10) it in place around the outer edge.

2 Sketch two eyelash shapes using a fabric pen, then backstitch over these lines.

3 Using freeform straight stitches, sew back and forth along the length of the lashes to shape them, thickening them at the base and making them taper off into a point.

highlights

Adding highlights to the eyes is one of my favorite parts of the whole dollmaking process: it's such a small step and takes only a few stitches, yet this is the moment that my characters come to life. Here are a few different options.

french knots

The perfect little stitch for a circular highlight (see page 11). Use one or two knots placed diagonally or in a straight line, and use more wraps around the needle to make one knot slightly bigger than the other.

straight stitches

Sometimes I like to use two small straight stitches under a French knot, arranged in a V-shape.

moons and stars

A few of the animals have pretty little crescent moon-shaped highlights in their eyes, with a tiny French knot (see page 11) as a star: I think it adds an air of mystery!

1 Draw a basic crescent shape onto the black felt eye, then using white floss (thread) and backstitch, outline the moon.

2 Using the same floss (thread), fill in this shape using rows of backstitch. Once the shape is filled in, use individual stitches to perfect the moon. Then simply add a French knot (see opposite).

tinting felt

This is another small, simple step that adds bags of character and dimension to a doll. It has become a bit of a tradition for me to add some rosy cheeks as the very last step in making my dolls: it is the perfect finishing touch. Tinting the inside of ears adds soft color and dimension to the shape.

Use an artists' soft pastel stick, pan pastel, or make-up blusher. If you are using make-up blusher, it should always be powder and not cream or gel-based, as it's very hard to blend those formulas evenly. Absorbent cotton (cotton wool) pads, cotton swabs (buds), and fingertips are the best tools for the job.

Always practice on a scrap piece of felt in the color that you will use. When making Juniper Bunny (see page 91), I swatched some bright pink and some peachy pink onto white felt, to check the blend quality and the intensity of the pigment, and I could try the swatch up against Juniper's face to see which color suited her best.

To add rosy cheeks, gently place a dot of color with your fingertip, then lightly blend it in with a cotton wool pad or cotton bud.

To tint ears, lay down some color, starting at the bottom center of the ear then blending it up and out. Go lightly and build up the color as you need it; the old adage "it's easier to add more than to take some away" is definitely true here.

making the basic doll

All the dolls in this book are made using the same basic pattern to create a doll that is approximately 14–15in (35–38cm) tall. If you want to make a doll that is smaller or larger, simply enlarge or reduce all the pattern pieces by the same amount, and adjust the fabric amounts accordingly.

body and limbs

1 Cut out all the doll body pieces from body-colored felt.

2 Begin by sewing the limbs. For the arms, place two arm pieces together and backstitch all around, leaving a turning gap of approximately ½in (1cm) on a straight edge. For the legs, sew all the way around, leaving a turning gap on a straight edge and leaving the top open.

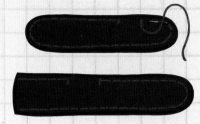

3 Turn each limb out the right way. Hemostats are a great tool for turning arms and legs; run the ends of the arms around the seams on the inside to push them out smoothly. Alternatively, you could use the rounded end of a pencil, or the wrong end of a knitting needle.

4 For the body, place the two body back pieces together and, taking a ¼in (5mm) seam allowance, backstitch them together along the straight edge, leaving a turning gap of around ¾in (2cm) in the lower part of the seam.

5 Next attach the legs to the body front, using just a few basting (tacking) stitches to hold them in place: these stitches won't be seen when the body is finished. The legs should extend past the body by approximately ¼in (5mm).

6 Fold the legs back on themselves so that they are within the edges of the body.

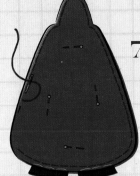

7 Now pin the back and front sections right sides together, so that the legs are in between the two pieces. Backstitch all around the edge.

8 Turn the doll out the right way by pulling the legs and then the rest of the body out through the turning gap in the back. Run the hemostats (haemostats) or the wrong end of a knitting needle around the inside of the seams to get a nice clean shape.

stuffing the doll

1 Stuff the legs, arms, and body through the turning gaps until they are fairly stiff.

2 Close all the turning gaps using ladder stitch (see page 11).

head

1 Make up the head following the instructions for the doll you are making. When you are sewing the front and back of the head together, leave the lower sides and bottom of the neck open.

2 Tuck the neck up inside the head (it will provide extra support when the head is fitted onto the body). Using ladder stitch, sew up a little of the neck hole, checking as you go until the head fits snugly onto the neck. Line the hole in the neck up directly under the mouth for good placement.

3 Place the head on the neck and use a few pins pushed through the base of the head into the neck to hold it firmly in place. Sew the head to the neck using ladder stitch all around.

arms

1 To attach the arms, you will need a doll needle (or any other long sewing needle). Use double thread and start by passing the thread through the shoulders a few times until the thread feels secure. Now add the arms; you will be sewing through an arm, the shoulders, and then the other arm, back and forth until the arms are very secure. Finish by adding a ¼in (6mm) button to each arm; these will keep the arms in position and stop them from loosening over time.

stuffing tips: It took me a while to realize how important the stuffing process is to a doll, and even the character of your doll—it's almost like sculpting. Here are my tips:

• Pull out a huge handful of stuffing onto your work surface, then nip off smaller handfuls depending on what you are filling. Gently tease a small ball of stuffing into a sausage shape; this will make it much easier to work with and gives a far better finish than trying to force a ball of stuffing through a small turning gap.

• Using the hemostats (haemostats), first push stuffing to the furthest part of the piece—for example, to the feet or the hands for the limbs.

• When stuffing limbs, stuff the foot/hand area quite firmly, continuing along the length and then stuffing a little less firmly at the top. When you add a strip of stuffing, push or tamp down the first part and feed the rest in, leaving the end quite loose and even poking out of the turning gap; then add the next strip of stuffing to it. This means that each strip will blend seamlessly into the next and you won't get lumps and bumps. (Note that the arms are attached with the closed turning gap at the back and not the top, so it won't be seen on your finished doll.)

• When stuffing the body, first lightly, evenly stuff the whole shape, using the same strip method but without tamping down the stuffing. Then pay attention to any small curves; roll small pieces of stuffing and use the hemostats to place them exactly where you want them, filling these areas fairly firmly, especially the neck and shoulder area. Move evenly around the body, filling it until it is quite firm.

• Stuff the head in the same way as the body. Once it is lightly stuffed, work around the top of the head filling the shape firmly, but it should be a softer fill around the neck opening. If you find that the seam around the top of the head is puckered, gently push into it with the stuffing and hemostats until you get the desired shape.

When filling one of the birds, bears, or the unicorn, the same principles apply. Fill the shape lightly and evenly at first, then go back and fill out the curves firmly.

clothes & accessories

Each project gives a list of the materials needed and the patterns to use to make the outfit the doll wears. Obviously you can choose your own colors and fabric prints for each garment, though it would be best to use the type of fabric suggested as that is what I have designed the items to be made from.

The patterns for all the garments and accessories can be found on pages 122–134, and on the following pages are instructions for making up each item.

sleeveless dress

Patterns are on page 133.

1 Use the patterns to cut out one front and two back bodices (note that all seam allowances are included in the patterns).

2 Snip into the curved seam allowance around the neckline on all the bodice pieces, turn it over to the wrong side, and secure the tabs with the glue pen. Also turn over and glue in place the small hem at the center back of each back bodice piece.

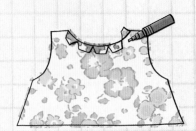

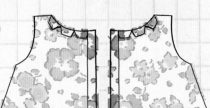

3 Using backstitch, sew around the necklines on the front and back pieces, and also down the straight hems at the center back.

4 Place the front bodice and one back bodice piece right sides together and backstitch the shoulder seam. Repeat to attach the other back bodice piece.

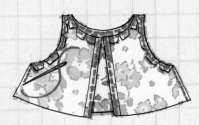

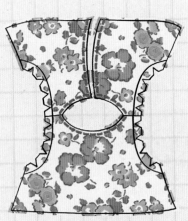

5 Open out the bodice and then snip into the curved seam allowance around each armhole. Turn them to the wrong side and secure the tabs with the glue pen.

6 Using backstitch, sew around the armholes. Without cutting the thread, place the bodice right sides together again and backstitch the side seams from the underarm to the waistline.

7 Cut a strip of fabric measuring 5 x 20in (13 x 50cm) for the skirt of the dress. Turn under a small hem at the right-hand short end. Place the bodice and the skirt right sides together with the bodice on top, lining up the bottom edge of the right-hand side of the bodice and the right-hand end of a long edge of the skirt. Start to backstitch the pieces together, taking a ⅛in (3mm) seam allowance. Fold small ¼in (5mm) pleats as you sew, with perhaps two or three stitches between each one. You may not need all 20in (50cm) of fabric, depending on how many pleats you put in (more pleats will give a fuller skirt). When you get toward the far end, turn under a small hem on the end of the skirt, then finish off the stitching. The short edges of the skirt can either be backstitched together along the hem fold lines, or you can glue each hem down and backstitch it in place, and leave the back of the skirt open. Turn under a hem along the bottom of the skirt and sew it with backstitch. Add two snap fasteners to the back of the bodice and sew on two ³⁄₁₆in (4mm) buttons to cover them.

boat-neck dress

Patterns are on page 130.

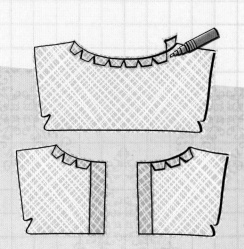

1 Use the patterns to cut out one front and two back bodices (note that all seam allowances are included in the patterns).

2 Snip into the curved seam allowance around the neckline on all the bodice pieces, turn it over to the wrong side, and secure the tabs with the glue pen. Also turn over and glue in place the small hem at the center back of each back bodice piece.

3 Using backstitch, sew around the necklines on the front and back pieces, and also down the straight hems at the center back.

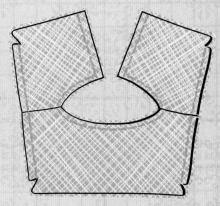

4 Place the front bodice and one back bodice piece right sides together and backstitch the shoulder seam. Repeat to attach the other back bodice piece.

5 Open out the bodice, turn under a small hem on each sleeve and secure it with the glue pen. Sew both sleeve hems using backstitch or running stitch.

6 Without cutting the thread, place the bodice right sides together again and backstitch the side seams from the underarm to the waistline.

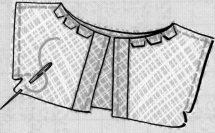

7 Add a skirt following Step 7 of the sleeveless dress (see above).

floaty-sleeve dress

Pattern is on page 131.

1 Use the patterns to cut out one front and two back bodices of the sleeveless dress (see page 133), and the floaty sleeve (note that all seam allowances are included in the patterns).

2 Follow Steps 2–4 of the sleeveless dress (see page 16) to make up the bodice.

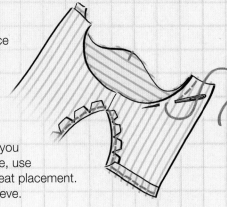

3 The size and shape of the sleeve allows for three pleats, one on either side of the shoulder seam and one in the center to line up with the shoulder seam. Mark the top center of each sleeve by folding it in half widthwise and pinching to make a small crease, or make a mark with a fabric pen.

4 Place one sleeve and the bodice right sides together, matching the top of the sleeve with the edge of the armhole. Use backstitch to start sewing the sleeve into the armhole, taking a 1/8in (3mm) seam allowance. When you get toward the top of the sleeve, use the center mark to help with pleat placement. Repeat to sew on the other sleeve.

5 Follow Steps 6–7 of the sleeveless dress to complete the floaty-sleeve dress.

v-neck dress

Patterns are on page 133.

1 Use the patterns to cut out two front and two back bodice pieces (note that all seam allowances are included in the patterns). Cutting the sloping edges with pinking shears will help to stop them fraying.

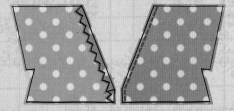

2 Fold in the seam allowances on the front pieces, glue them in place, then backstitch along each edge.

3 Overlap the two front pieces by a very small amount and sew them together with a few straight stitches.

4 Snip into the curved seam allowance around the neckline on the back bodice pieces, turn it over to the wrong side, and secure the tabs with the glue pen. Also turn over and glue in place the small hem at the center back of each back bodice piece.

5 Follow Steps 4–7 of the boat-neck dress to complete the v-neck dress (see page 17).

jeans and shorts

Pattern is on page 133.

1 Use the pattern to cut out two jeans or shorts pieces (note that all seam allowances are included in the patterns).

2 Pin the pieces right sides together. First, backstitch around the inner legs, then make tiny snips around the top of the inner leg seam allowance to give a nice smooth shape when turned right-side out.

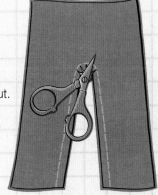

3 Now backstitch down both the side seams of the jeans.

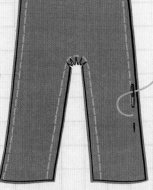

4 Turn under a ¼in (5mm) hem all around the waist and backstitch it in place. Try the jeans on your doll for fit. Make two pleats or folds in the back to give a nice smooth shape at the front and a good fit at the waist. Mark these folds with a fabric pen and remove the jeans from the doll. Add a snap fastener to the inside of each fold.

Alternatively, you could add some fine elastic to make a gathered waist, as if you were making the doll underwear (see page 26).

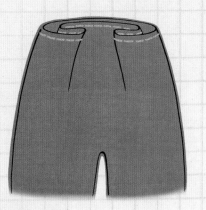

5 Turn the jeans right side out and either turn under and backstitch a narrow hem around the bottom of each leg, or make turn-ups, folding the fabric over twice to hide the raw edges.

shirt

Patterns are on page 132.

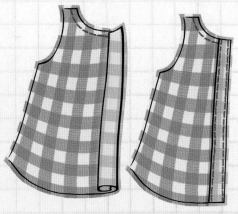

1 Use the patterns to cut out the two fronts, one back, two sleeves, and two collars—if a collar is required (note that all seam allowances are included in the patterns).

2 Fold under and backstitch a small hem around the neckline of each shirt front. To make the button plackets, turn a double ¼in (5mm) hem to the right side of the fabric. Backstitch a line up each side of both plackets.

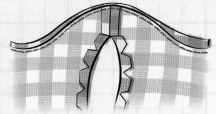

3 Place one shirt front and the back piece right sides together and backstitch the shoulder seam. Repeat to attach the other shirt front piece..

4 Place one sleeve and the shirt body right sides together, matching the top of the sleeve with the edge of the armhole. Use backstitch to sew the sleeve into the armhole, taking a ⅛in (3mm) seam allowance. Repeat to sew on the other sleeve.

5 Place the front and back of the shirt right sides together again, lining up the sleeves and sides. Sew along the sleeve from the cuff to the underarm and from the underarm down the side of the shirt. Repeat for the other side, then turn the shirt right side out.

6 To add a collar to the shirt, snip into the seam allowance of the two curved sides of the collar pieces, then fold them to the wrong side and secure the tabs with the glue pen. Backstitch around both edges. Do not fold in the seam allowance along the top of the collar, as you will use this to stitch the collar to the neckline.

7 Place one collar at the neckline, pointing upward, so that the right side of the shirt and the wrong side of the collar are facing you. Match the seam line of the collar with the edge of the neckline, then backstitch along the seam allowance, making sure that you catch the neckline in the stitches to sew the pieces together. Then fold the collar down the right way. Repeat with the other collar piece on the other front.

8 Turn under a hem around the bottom edge of the shirt and backstitch it in place.

9 Turn up the sleeves, folding the fabric over twice to hide the raw edges. If you want short sleeves, you may find it best to trim the sleeves a bit shorter to reduce bulk when turning them up.

10 Add snap fasteners to the front of the shirt, and four or five ³⁄₁₆in (4mm) buttons down one placket.

t-shirt

Patterns are on page 134.

1 Use the patterns to cut out one front, two backs, and two sleeves (note that all seam allowances are included in the patterns).

2 Follow Steps 1–6 of the boat-neck dress (see page 17) to make up the t-shirt. Turn under and backstitch a hem around the bottom of the t-shirt.

smock top

Patterns are on page 133.

1 Use the patterns to cut out the front and back bodice pieces (note that all seam allowances are included in the patterns).

2 Follow Steps 1–6 of the boat-neck dress (see page 17) to make up the smock bodice. Sew a length of trim in place around each armhole.

3 Cut a strip of fabric measuring 20 x 3½in (50 x 9cm) for the skirt of the smock, then make up the skirt as for the boat-neck dress.

cape

Patterns are on page 131.

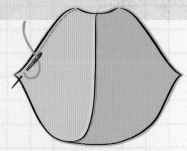

1 Use the patterns to cut out two cape fronts, one cape back, two collar fronts, and one collar back (note that all seam allowances are included in the patterns).

2 Pin the cape back and one cape front piece right sides together. Starting at the neckline and using backstitch, sew along the shoulder and down the side. Repeat to sew the second cape front to the other side of the back.

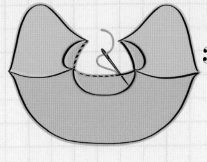

3 Turn the cape right side and attach the collar pieces using whip stitch.

4 Using running stitch or blanket stitch—whichever you prefer—sew all around the edges of the cape, including around the edges of the collar.

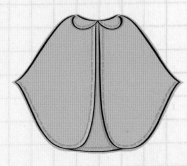

stole

Pattern is on page 132.

1 Use the pattern to cut one stole piece (note that all seam allowances are included in the pattern).

2 Sew a decorative line of running stitch or backstitch around the edge of the stole. The stole can be left just like this, or you can add more embroidery, decorate it with buttons, pearls, or even add a mini rose (see page 25).

3 Cut three lengths of embroidery floss (thread), each measuring 6in (15cm). Knot the three lengths together at one end and pin this knot to a pincushion. Braid (plait) the strands together until the braid (plait) measures 3–4in (8–10cm) long. Knot the floss (thread) to secure the braid (plait), then trim the ends of the floss to make a neat tassel. Make a second braid (plait) to match the first one.

4 With a few straight stitches, sew one end of each braid (plait) to the front underside of the stole. Be careful to position them at the same point on each side so that the stole sits neatly when the braids (plaits) are tied together.

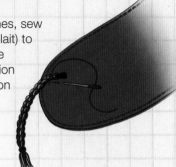

bolero

Patterns are on page 131.

1 Use the patterns to cut out two fronts and one back (note that all seam allowances are included in the patterns). If possible with the lace you have, arrange the pieces on the lace so that the bottom edge of each piece is the finished edge of the lace, so creating a scalloped or shaped hem (see page 80).

2 Follow Steps 1–6 of boat-neck dress (see page 17) to make up the bolero, bearing in mind that the opening is center front, not center back as for the dress.

blazer

Patterns are on page 132.

1 Use the patterns to cut out two backs, four fronts, two sleeves, and two pockets (note that all seam allowances are included in the patterns).

2 Turn under the seam allowances around the edges of the blazer pockets, apart from the top edge. Backstitch the turned edges in place.

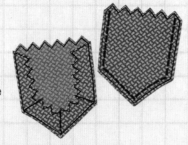

3 Place one pocket on the right side of one blazer front, pointing upward and with the wrong side facing you. Backstitch across the seam line of the top edge. You can fold the pocket down and press it in place once the blazer is finished. Repeat to attach a pocket to a second blazer front.

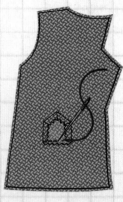

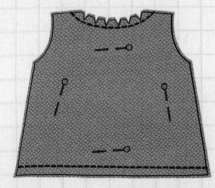

4 Pin a blazer front with a pocket and a plain front right sides together. Backstitch along the bottom, up the front, and around the lapel and neckline up to the shoulder.

5 Snip into the seam allowance at the neckline and the inner corners of the lapel, then snip off the outer corners and turn the front blazer piece right side out. Repeat to make a second front.

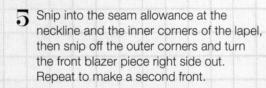

6 Pin the two back blazer pieces right sides together. Backstitch around the neckline and along the bottom hem. Snip into the seam allowance at the neckline and turn the piece right side out.

7 Place one of the front blazer pieces right sides together with the back piece. Backstitch across the shoulder. Repeat to sew the other front piece to the back.

8 The size and shape of the sleeve allows for three pleats, one on either side of the shoulder seam and one in the center to line up with the shoulder seam. Mark the top center of each sleeve by folding it in half widthwise and pinching to make a small crease, or make a mark with a fabric pen.

9 Place one sleeve and the blazer body right sides together, matching the top of the sleeve with the edge of the armhole. Use backstitch to start sewing the sleeve into the armhole, taking a ⅛in (3mm) seam allowance. When you get toward the top of the sleeve, use the center mark to help with pleat placement. Repeat to sew on the other sleeve.

10 Turn under a small hem at each cuff and backstitch it in place.

11 Place the front and the back of the blazer right sides together and line up the sleeves and the sides. Pin in place and sew along the sleeves from the cuff to the armhole and from the armhole down the side of the blazer, making sure to stitch through all four layers of fabric. Repeat for the other side of the blazer. Turn right side out.

12 Fold back the lapels and fold down the pockets, then gently press the blazer with a warm to medium iron. If your blazer fabric needs a hotter iron, then lay a scrap piece of cotton on top before pressing.

denim jacket

Patterns are on page 131.

1 Use the patterns to cut out two fronts, two backs, two collars, two sleeves, two pockets, and two faux seams (note that all seam allowances are included in the patterns).

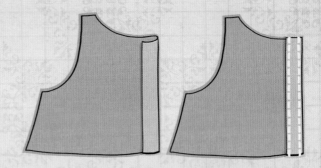

2 Snip into the curved seam allowance around the neckline on both front pieces, turn it over to the wrong side, and secure the tabs with the glue pen. Fold over a narrow double hem down the edge of each front, folding it to the right side. Secure it with the glue pen, then backstitch a line down both edges of the hem.

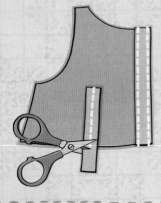

3 Spread some glue on the wrong side of each faux seam strip, then fold both raw edges into the centre. Add some more glue and stick one strip to each front of the denim jacket, allowing the lower end to overlap the bottom edge of the jacket. Backstitch a line down each strip, then trim off the excess.

4 Turn in the seam allowances around the edges of both pockets and secure them with the glue pen. Backstitch across the top of one pocket, then, without cutting the thread, backstitch 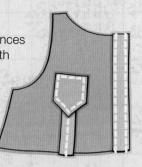 the pocket in place onto the front of the denim jacket: the point of the pocket should overlap the faux seam by a tiny amount. Repeat to sew the other pocket to the other jacket front.

5 Work Steps 6–9 of the blazer (see pages 23–24).

6 Snip into the seam allowance of the two curved sides of the collar pieces, then fold them to the wrong side and secure the tabs with the glue pen. Backstitch around both edges. Do not fold in the seam allowance along the top of the collar, as you will use this to stitch the collar to the neckline.

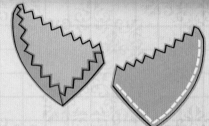

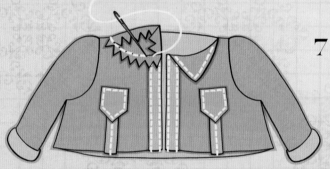

7 Place one collar at the neckline, pointing upward, so that the right side of the shirt and the wrong side of the collar are facing you. Match the seam line of the collar with the edge of the neckline, then backstitch along the seam allowance making sure that you catch the neckline in the stitches to sew the pieces together. Then fold the collar down the right way. Repeat with the other collar piece on the other front.

rose

Patterns are on page 131.

1 Use the patterns to cut out the rose curl and some extra petals (if needed, see Step 3).

2 Starting at one end, simply roll the rose up. Keep the base flat and once the curl is completely rolled, secure it with a pin pushed right through the base. Stitch through all the layers so that the rose doesn't unravel. These stitches won't be seen, so the aim here is to secure all the layers.

3 If you think your rose needs a few extra individual petals to round its shape out or to even it up, then just cut out as many as are needed and attach them using whip stitch. Similarly, you can cut simple leaf shapes and sew those to the back of the rose.

underwear

Pattern is on page 133.

1 Use the pattern to cut out two pieces (note that all seam allowances are included in the pattern).

2 Place the two pieces right sides together. Sew the gusset (this will only take a few stitches), then sew down either side of the underwear.

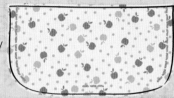

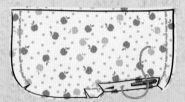

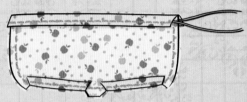

3 To finish the leg holes, make small diagonal snips into the fabric where the stitching starts and ends and then turn under a hem. Sew around each leg hole using running stitch or backstitch.

4 Turn under a ¼in (5mm) hem around the waistline and place some fine elastic in it. Stitch all around using running stitch or backstitch: be careful not to catch the elastic with your needle or to sew through it. Before you finish sewing around the waist, try the underwear on your doll, pull the elastic to gather the waist to fit, and tie it in a double knot. Remove the underwear, trim the elastic, and finish sewing the hem closed.

clutch purse

Pattern is on page 132.

1 Use the pattern to cut out one piece (note that all seam allowances are included in the pattern).

2 Fold the purse so that the pointed flap overlaps the front. Use hemostats to press the folds in place to create the shape of the purse.

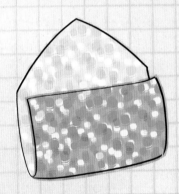

3 Sew the snap fastener in place using a fine needle and strong thread. Sew a line of backstitch across the square edge of the purse front and around the flap.

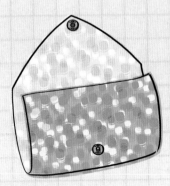

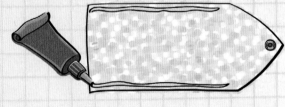

4 Open the purse out again, run a line of fabric glue along each long straight side, and re-fold the purse. Hold the layers together for a minute or so until the glue dries.

shoulder purse

Patterns are on page 132.

1 Use the patterns to cut out one front, one back, and one strap (note that all seam allowances are included in the patterns).

2 Place the purse front and back wrong sides together, matching the rounded edges. Whip stitch around these edges.

3 Stitch one half of the snap fastener to the underside of the flap and at the same time add the toggle to the outside. Stitch the other half of the snap fastener to the main body of the purse, lining the pieces up carefully to make sure the placement is correct.

4 Fold the purse strap in half lengthwise and glue the layers together. Backstitch along the length.

5 Stitch one end of the purse strap to one side of the purse using a few straight stitches. Repeat on the other side.

shoes

Patterns are on page 134.

All the shoes are made using the following instructions.

1 Use the patterns to cut out two shoe uppers and two soles (note that all seam allowances are included in the patterns). For boots, cut out four identical pieces.

2 If you want to add detail to the shoe upper, backstitch around any cut out sections.

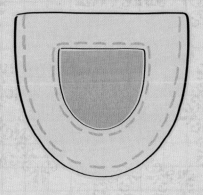

3 Put one upper and one sole wrong sides together, matching the edges. Whip stitch the pieces together, leaving the top open. Without cutting the thread, backstitch around the top edge if required.

4 Customize each pair of shoes to suit your doll, stitch on small buttons as fasteners, glue on flat back pearls, or just like Maddie the Elephant (see page 67), glue on some tiny glittery hearts.

socks

Pattern is on page 134.

1 Cut four sock pieces from stretch jersey fabric. Turn under a small hem on the straight edge of each one and backstitch it in place.

2 Place two pieces right sides together and backstitch the pieces together, leaving the top open. Repeat to make a second sock.

chapter 1

in the trees

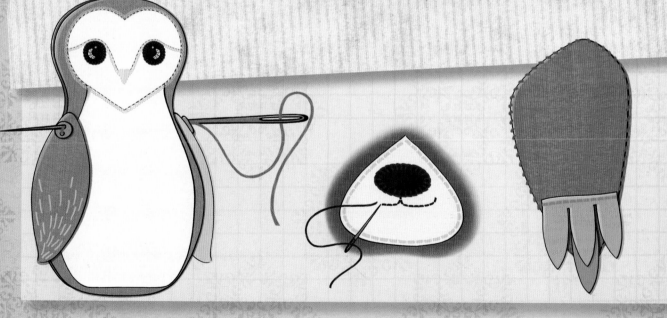

you will need

Basic body templates on page 122

Koala bear head, face, and ear templates on page 125

V-neck dress pattern on page 133

Underwear pattern on page 133

Peep-toe shoe pattern on page 134

Clutch bag pattern on page 132

19¼ x 13in (49 x 33cm) of marled gray felt for body, head, outer ears, arms, and legs

2¾ x 3in (7 x 8cm) of white felt for inner ears

2 x 3½in (5 x 9cm) of black felt for eyes and nose

3 x 3in (8 x 8cm) of felt for shoes

20 x 8in (50 x 20cm) of cotton fabric for dress

3½ x 2½in (9 x 6cm) of faux leather for clutch purse

5½ x 5¼in (14 x 13cm) of cotton fabric for underwear

Basic sewing kit (see page 8)

Embroidery floss (thread) to match each felt color, dress, underwear, and bag

Glue pen

3 x snap fasteners

2 x flat-back pearls

Peachy-pink pastel or blusher

About 2oz (55g) of toy stuffing

Aren't koalas the most adorable? With their quirky noses and beautiful big round ears, I can't get enough of them! Pearl is looking very sweet and elegant in her V-neck polka dot dress, faux leather clutch, and pearl-embellished peep-toe shoes. Perhaps she is off for afternoon tea with some of her friends.

cutting out and making the doll's body

Using the templates for the basic body, cut out, sew, and assemble Pearl's body and limbs, following the instructions on page 14.

face

1 Cut two heads and four outer ears from gray felt. Cut two inner ears from white felt. Cut two eyes and both the koala nose pieces from black felt.

2 Using the glue pen, stick the koala nose pieces together, with piece 2 on top of piece 1. Backstitch the nostrils only, making sure you are sewing both layers of felt together. Don't cut the floss (thread).

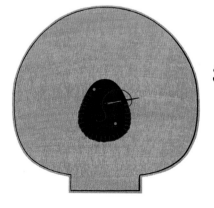

3 Place the nose on one of the koala head pieces and secure with the glue pen or some pins. Stitch the nose to the face all around the outside edge using blanket stitch.

4 Using the photographs as a guide, sew the eyes in place with blanket stitch and embroider eyelashes using some free-form straight stitches. Finish the eyes by adding a few highlights with white floss (thread) (page 12 has ideas and advice for embroidering lashes and highlights).

head

1 Pin the front and the back of the head right sides together and backstitch all around the outer edge, leaving the neck area open (see page 15).

2 Turn the head right side out, push out the seams, and stuff it (page 15 has more advice on stuffing a doll).

ears

1 Place an inner ear onto an outer ear and hold it in place with the glue pen or some pins. Backstitch the layers together around the curved edge.

2 Place the stitched outer ear right sides together with a plain outer ear and backstitch all around the curved edge, leaving the bottom edge open. Repeat to make a second ear.

3 Turn each ear right side out and press the seam out to get a smooth curve.

4 Place an ear on either side of the head, positioning them so that the ends of the ear seam touch the head seam. Separate the front and back layers just a little so that the ear straddles the seam. Secure each ear with a few pins pushed through the base of the ear and down into the head.

5 Ladder stitch all around the base of each ear.

attaching the doll's head

Follow the instructions on page 15 to attach Pearl's head to her body. Add a little color to the cheeks using the pastel or blusher (turn to page 13 for more about tinting felt).

clothes and accessories

All the clothes patterns are on pages 130–134.

Pearl's polka dot cotton dress is made using the V-neck dress pattern.

Make the pretty peep-toe shoes from felt, then attach a flat-back pearl to the toe-bar of each one.

Pearl's underwear is made from thin cotton fabric.

Her clutch purse is made from faux leather fabric.

alfie the red panda

The red panda is sometimes known as the red bear cat or the fire fox, and their bold face markings and jaunty eyebrows give them lots of character. Alfie is wearing a cool stripy t-shirt, but you could easily make a plain white tee and add a motif, or embroider a word, a quote, or a name.

you will need

Basic body templates on page 122

Red panda head, face, and ear templates on page 130

T-shirt pattern on page 134

Shorts pattern on page 133

Boots pattern on page 134

16 x 10in (40 x 25cm) of rust felt for head, outer ears, and body

10¼ x 8¾in (26 x 22cm) of black felt for arms, legs, eyes, nose, and small inner ear

4 x 5½in (10 x 14cm) of white felt for muzzle, face markings, eyebrows, and larger inner ears

11 x 9in (28 x 23cm) of stretch jersey for t-shirt

10 x 5½in (25 x 14cm) of denim chambray for shorts

4 x 3in (10 x 8cm) of felt for boots

Basic sewing kit (see page 8)

Embroidery floss (threads) to match each felt color, and t-shirt and shorts fabrics

Glue pen

3 x snap fasteners

About 2oz (55g) of toy stuffing

cutting out and making the doll's body

Using the templates for the basic body, cut out, stitch, and assemble Alfie's body and limbs, following the instructions on page 14.

face

1 Cut two heads and four outer ears from rust-colored felt. Cut two inner ears, one muzzle, two eyebrows, and two face patches from white felt. Cut two eyes, two small inner ears, and one nose from black felt.

2 As there are lots of elements to the red panda's face, it is a good idea to work out the placement of each piece before starting sewing. So arrange all the features on one of the head pieces and adjust them until you are happy with how everything looks. Then glue down the muzzle, the two curved face markings, and the two white eyebrows. Backstitch around each shape.

3 Add the eyes and nose and blanket stitch around them. Finish the eyes by adding a few highlights with white floss (thread) – (page 12 has ideas and advice for embroidering highlights).

attaching the doll's head

Once you've finished Alfie's face and ears, follow the instructions on page 15 to attach his head to his body.

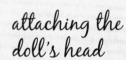

4 For the red panda's mouth, draw two slightly curved lines that extend down from the bottom center of the nose. Backstitch over these lines.

5 Pin the front and the back of the head right sides together and backstitch all around the outer edge, leaving the neck area open (see page 15). Turn the head right side out, push out the seams, and stuff it (page 15 has more advice on stuffing a doll).

ears

1 Place a white inner ear onto an outer ear and hold it in place with glue or some pins. Backstitch the layers together around the curved edge but leave the base open.

2 Glue the black small inner ear into place and backstitch around the top, but not across the base.

3 Place the stitched outer ear right sides together with a plain outer ear and backstitch all around the curved edge, leaving the bottom edge open. Repeat to make a second ear. Turn each ear right side out and press the seam out to get a smooth curve.

4 Place an ear on either side of the head, positioning them so that the ends of the ear seam touch the head seam. Separate the front and back layers just a little so that the ear straddles the seam. Secure each ear with a few pins pushed through the base of the ear and down into the head. Ladder stitch all around the base of each ear.

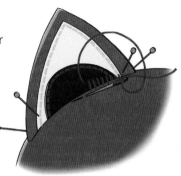

clothes and accessories

All the clothes patterns are on pages 130–134.

Alfie's striped t-shirt is made from a light-weight jersey fabric.

His knee-length shorts are made from chambray fabric.

Alfie's boots are light brown felt.

Tip: You can always use your own old clothes to make Alfie's outfit. His t-shirt is made from the sleeves of one of my own t-shirts that I had kept in my fabric stash just waiting for the right little character to come along.

you will need

Basic body templates on page 122

Sloth head and face templates on page 123

Boat-neck dress pattern on page 130

Underwear pattern on page 133

T-bar shoe pattern on page 134

15 x 15½in (38 x 39cm) of caramel-colored felt for body, arms, legs, and head

5¼ x 4in (13 x 10cm) of white felt for face

1½ x 1¼in (4 x 3cm) of black felt for eyes and nose

2½ x 2¾in (6 x 7cm) of brown felt for eye patches

3 x 3in (8 x 8cm) of felt for shoes

20 x 8¼in (50 x 21cm) of denim chambray for dress

5½ x 5¼in (14 x 13cm) of cotton fabric for underwear

Basic sewing kit (see page 8)

Embroidery floss (threads) to match each felt color, dress, and underwear, plus red, yellow, orange, and green for the floral embroidery

Glue pen

2 x snap fasteners

8–10 x small flat-back pearls

Peachy-pink pastel or blusher

About 2oz (55g) of toy stuffing

Sloths are such wonderfully quirky creatures, and they always seem to be smiling. My little Abbi is certainly very happy indeed with her brand-new embroidered dress. Have fun personalizing her outfit, add more flowers, leaves, and pearls, or add some different motifs–stars or geometric shapes perhaps?

cutting out and making the doll's body

Using the templates for the basic body, cut out, sew, and assemble Abbi's body and limbs, following the instructions on page 14.

face

1 Cut two heads from caramel felt. Cut one face from white felt. Cut two eye patches from brown felt. Cut two eyes and one nose from black felt.

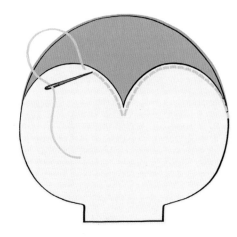

2 Lay the face panel onto one of the head pieces and hold it in place with glue or pins. Backstitch around the top, sewing through both layers. Do not sew around the cheeks or neck.

3 Lay the two eye patch pieces in place, angling them both down slightly as shown. They should extend ¼in (6mm) beyond the edge of the head. Sew them in place using backstitch or blanket stitch around the edges.

4 Using the photographs as a guide, sew on the eyes and the nose using a blanket stitch all around the edges. Add a few highlights in the eyes using French knots (page 12 has ideas and advice for embroidering highlights).

5 Draw a short vertical line beneath the nose and two slightly curved lines for the mouth, and embroider them using backstitch.

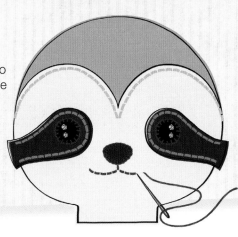

head

1 Pin the front and the back of the head right sides together and backstitch all around the outer edge, leaving the neck area open (see page 15).

2 Turn the head right side out, push out the seams, and stuff it (page 15 has more advice on stuffing a doll).

attaching the doll's head

Follow the instructions on page 15 to attach Abbi's head to her body. Add a little color to the cheeks using the pastel or blusher (turn to page 13 for more about tinting felt).

clothes and accessories

All the clothes patterns are on pages 130–134.
Make Abbi's dress using the boat-neck dress pattern.

French knot

Pearl placement

Satin stitch

Lazy daisy

Herringbone stitch

Woven wheel stitch

Tip: Denim chambray is a great fabric for making doll jeans and other denim doll garments. It is so much softer and finer than real denim that it is much easier to stitch tiny hems, seams, and other details.

Tip: Embroidering such tiny flowers can seem a little fiddly at first, but it comes together quite quickly and looks so impressive when you are finished. Remember to use a fine needle and one strand of embroidery floss (thread).

Using the illustration above as a guide, sketch some flower shapes and dots onto the shoulders of the dress. Embroider them with the various stitches shown, referring to the stitches on pages 10–11 and to widely available embroidery instructions on the internet.

Add a few small flat-back pearls with some tweezers and a tiny amount of fabric glue.

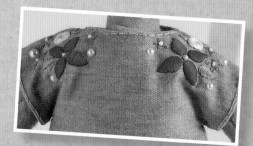

Abbi's T-bar shoes each have a little pearl glued on as a button.

Her underwear is made from thin cotton fabric.

stevie the raccoon

Intelligent, curious, and perhaps just a little bit mischievous, the beloved raccoon has human-like hands that get them into all sorts of trouble—they have been known to open bottles, doors, and even trash cans. But our Stevie is behaving herself today, showing off her pretty red cape embellished with a tiny rose and her cute tan boots that are perfect for running around in the woods.

you will need

- Basic body templates on page 122
- Raccoon head, face, and ear templates on page 130
- Sleeveless dress pattern on page 133
- Boots pattern on page 134
- Underwear pattern on page 133
- Cape pattern on page 131
- 14¾ x 16in (37 x 40cm) of charcoal-gray felt for body, arms, legs, head, and ears
- 5½ x 4in (14 x 10cm) of white felt for muzzle, inner ears, and larger eye patches
- 4 x 3in (10 x 8cm) of black felt for nose, eyes, and smaller eye patches
- 10¼ x 7in (26 x 18cm) of felt for cape
- 3 x 3in (8 x 8cm) of felt for rose
- ¾ x ¾in (2 x 2cm) of felt for leaves
- 4 x 3in (10 x 8cm) of felt for boots
- 20 x 8in (50 x 20cm) of cotton fabric for dress
- 5½ x 5¼in (14 x 13cm) of cotton fabric for underwear
- Basic sewing kit (see page 8)
- Embroidery floss (threads) to match each felt color, dress, and underwear
- Glue pen
- 2 x snap fasteners
- About 2oz (55g) of toy stuffing

cutting out and making the doll's body

Using the templates for the basic body, cut out, stitch, and assemble Stevie's body and limbs, following the instructions on page 14.

face

1 Cut two heads and four outer ears from charcoal-gray felt. Cut two inner ears, two larger eye patches, and one muzzle from white felt. Cut eyes, two smaller eye patches, and one nose from black felt.

2 As there are lots of elements to the raccoon's face, it is a good idea to work out the placement of each piece before starting sewing. So arrange all the features on one of the head pieces and adjust them until you are happy with how everything looks. Then glue down the white eye patches and the muzzle: the ends of the eye patches should extend past the head by about ¼in (6mm). Backstitch around each piece.

attaching the doll's head

Once you've finished Stevie's face and ears, follow the instructions on page 15 to attach her head to her body.

3 Glue the black eye patches over the top of the white ones, lining them up so that no white shows along the lower edge, then either blanket stitch or whip stitch them in place.

4 Sew the eyes and nose in place with blanket stitch. Finish the eyes by adding a few highlights with white floss (thread) (page 12 has ideas and advice for embroidering lashes and highlights). Add a highlight to the nose.

Tip: The raccoon's dark eye patches frame their glossy dark eyes, but if you find this is all too dark, you could always outline the eyes—or the outer half of the eyes—with a mid- to light-toned gray floss (thread), to make their eyes really stand out!

5 For the mouth draw a ¼in (6mm) line extending down from the bottom center of the nose, then draw a slightly curved line under this. Backstitch over these lines.

6 Pin the front and the back of the head right sides together and backstitch all around the outer edge, leaving the neck area open (see page 15). Turn the head right side out, push out the seams, and stuff it (page 15 has more advice on stuffing a doll).

ears

1 Place an inner ear onto an outer ear and hold it in place with glue or some pins. Backstitch the layers together around the curved edge but leave the base unstitched.

2 Place the stitched outer ear right sides together with a plain outer ear and backstitch all around the curved edge, leaving the bottom edge open. Repeat to make a second ear. Turn each ear right side out and press the seam out to get a smooth shape.

3 Place an ear on either side of the head, positioning them so that the ends of the ear seam touch the head seam. Separate the front and back layers just a little so that the ear straddles the seam. Secure each ear with a few pins pushed through the base of the ear and down into the head. Ladder stitch all around the base of each ear.

clothes and accessories

All the clothes patterns are on pages 130–134.

Stevie's sleeveless dress is made in cotton with a tiny floral print.

Stevie's cape is embellished with a simple running stitch in a contrasting color floss (thread).

Cut two simple leaf shapes and sew them to the back of the rose.

Stevie's boots are quick and simple to sew.

Tip: There are many different ways to embellish Stevie's cape; try a different flower or some embroidery, or maybe you have a broken earring or other piece of jewelry that you could use as a brooch or a clasp.

joni the barn owl

I have always admired the barn owl's heart-shaped face, big round eyes, and soft coloring. There is huge scope here for you to add more details and embellishments to your own Joni. Try adding extra French knots, lazy daisy stitches, or more lines of chain stitch to represent the flecks and texture of the feathers.

you will need

Bird body and base templates on page 124

Owl belly, face, and wing templates on page 124

19 x 13½in (48 x 34cm) of light brown felt for body, base, and outer wings

6¼ x 5¼in (16 x 13cm) of light caramel-colored felt for inner wings

10½ x 10½in (27 x 27cm) of white felt for face/belly panel, face, and brow

2½ x 1¼in (6 x 3cm) of black felt for eyes

¾ x ¾in (2 x 2cm) of light pink felt for beak

Basic sewing kit (see page 8)

Embroidery floss (threads) to match each felt color, plus pale beige and warm brown

Glue pen

White fabric pencil

Fabric glue

2 x ¼in (6mm) buttons to attach wings

Peachy-pink pastel or blusher

About 4oz (110g) of toy stuffing

cutting out the doll

Cut out two bodies, one base, and two wings from light brown felt. Cut two wings from caramel felt. Cut one face/belly panel, one face, and one brow from white felt. Cut two eyes from black felt. Cut one beak from light pink felt.

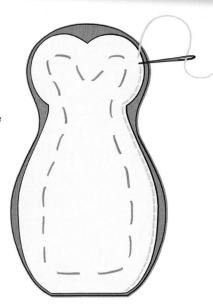

face

1 Baste (tack) the face/belly piece onto one of the owl body pieces, then backstitch all around the edge of the white panel. When sewing around the face section of the panel, your stitches can be a little bigger than usual as they will be covered by the face panel. Remove the basting (tacking) stitches.

Tip: As the face/belly panel is quite big, I choose to secure it with basting (tacking) stitches instead of using a glue pen. It would require a lot of glue to hold it in place, but basting (tacking) stitches will hold it firmly, and they won't get in the way as pins sometimes can.

2 Lay the brow piece on top of the face piece and pin or glue it in place. Whip stitch around the lower edge of the brow.

3 Add the eyes just under the brow and blanket stitch all around the edges of them.

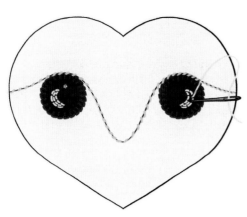

4 Using the white fabric pencil, lightly sketch the crescent moon shape onto the eyes. Outline the moon shape with backstitch, then fill in the shape using rows of straight stitches. Add a white French knot using doubled embroidery floss (thread) to make a larger knot (page 12 has ideas and advice for embroidering highlights).

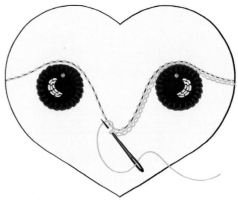

5 Using a light beige and doubled embroidery floss (thread), chain stitch along the line of the brow to add some gentle definition.

6 Put some fabric glue onto the back of the beak and pinch down the middle of it lengthwise to create a crease. Let the glue dry so that the beak holds the shape, then whip stitch the beak in place using small stitches.

7 Now lay the whole face panel in position over the top of the face/belly panel, and hold it in place with pins or basting (tacking) stitches. Whip stitch all around the heart-shaped face to sew all the layers together. Then using a warm brown floss (thread), chain stitch all around the face.

body

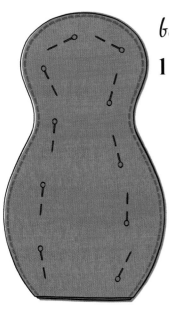

1 Pin the front and back body pieces right sides together and backstitch around the sides and the head, leaving the base open.

2 Turn the body right side out and stuff it. Stuff the head and body quite firmly, but leave the very bottom of the body only lightly filled for now; as you sew in the base you can add more stuffing to make it firm (page 15 has more advice on stuffing a doll).

3 Turn the owl upside down and place the base over the opening at the bottom. Use ladder stitch to sew the base to the body all the way around. Add more toy stuffing as you go, but don't over-stuff or the base will become rounded and the owl won't stand up straight.

wings

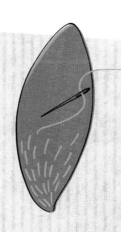

1 On each of the outer wings, use two strands of embroidery floss (thread) in a light beige color to make random straight stitches to represent feathers. Embroider the lower third of each wing, spacing the stitches out a bit as you work upward.

2 Place one outer wing and one inner wing right sides together and backstitch all around, leaving a gap of about ½in (12mm).

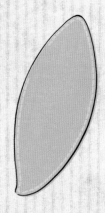

3 Turn the wing out the right way and close the gap with a ladder stitch. No need to stuff the wings for this bird. Repeat to make a second wing.

4 Add the wings in much the same way as adding the doll arms (see page 15). Use a long doll needle and sew back and forth through the arms and the body, adding buttons at the end for extra security. Add a little color to the cheeks using the pastel or blusher (turn to page 13 for more about tinting felt).

Tip: There is plenty of room on Joni for you to add lots more embroidery if you want to; add lines of chain stitch on her belly, or stitch some pretty lazy-daisy stitch flowers. Or perhaps embroider the name or initial of someone special.

Jenny the panda

Pandas are one of the world's most adored animals; how could you not love them? The gentle nature of the panda is traditionally a symbol of peace and harmony. However, if you have ever seen a baby panda in action you will know that they are very playful and very funny, not to mention cute! Jenny's pretty felt stole can be embellished in all sorts of ways—add ribbon ties, beads, embroidery, or buttons.

cutting out and making the doll's body

Using the templates for the basic body, cut out, stitch, and assemble Jenny's body and limbs, following the instructions on page 14.

face

1 Cut two heads from white felt. Cut two eye patches, four ears, and one nose from dark gray felt. Cut two eyes from black felt.

2 Glue the eye patches and nose to one of the head pieces, then backstitch around the edges of each feature. Using a fabric marker, draw a ¼in (5mm) line down from the bottom center of the nose, then two slightly curved lines extending out from it in either direction. Backstitch over these lines with dark gray floss (thread).

3 Using the photographs as a guide, sew the eyes in place with blanket stitch. Finish the eyes by adding a few highlights with white floss (thread) (page 12 has ideas and advice for embroidering highlights).

4 Pin the front and the back of the head right sides together and backstitch all around the outer edge, leaving the neck area open (see page 15). Turn the head right side out, push out the seams, and stuff it (page 15 has more advice on stuffing a doll).

ears

1 Place two ear pieces right sides together and backstitch the layers together around the curved edge, leaving the base of the ear open. Repeat to make a second ear. Turn each ear right side out and press the seam out to get a smooth curve.

2 Place an ear on either side of the head, positioning them so that the ends of the ear seam touch the head seam. Separate the front and back layers just a little so that the ear straddles the seam. Secure each ear with a few pins pushed through the base of the ear and down into the head.

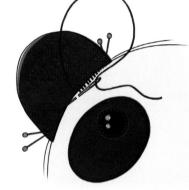

3 Ladder stitch all around the base of each ear.

clothes and accessories

All the clothes patterns are on pages 130–134.

Jenny's boat-neck dress is made in floral cotton.

Her felt stole is edged with blanket stitch.

Jenny's underwear is made from thin cotton fabric.

Jenny's Mary Jane shoes are made in purple felt to complement the flower centers on her dress.

attaching the doll's head

Follow the instructions on page 15 to attach Jenny's head to her body. Add a little color to the cheeks using the pastel or blusher (turn to page 13 for more about tinting felt).

you will need

Basic doll templates on page 122

Monkey head, muzzle, nose, eye, and ear templates on page 128

Smock pattern on page 133

Mary Jane shoe pattern on page 134

Underwear pattern on page 133

14½ x 16¼in (37 x 41cm) of brown felt for body, arms, legs, head, and outer ears

4 x 5½in (10 x 14cm) of caramel-colored felt for face, muzzle, and inner ears

1¼ x ¾in (3 x 2cm) of black felt for eyes

3 x 3in (8 x 8cm) of felt for shoes

20 x 6in (50 x 15cm) of cotton fabric for smock top

Approximately 20in (50cm) of ruffle trim

5½ x 5¼in (14 x 13cm) of cotton fabric for shorts

3 x 3in (8 x 8cm) of felt for rose

Basic sewing kit (see page 8)

Embroidery floss (thread) to match each felt color, top, and shorts

Glue pen

2 x snap fasteners

Peachy-pink pastel or blusher

Approximately 2oz (55g) of toy stuffing

rooni the monkey

Now I know that monkeys are renowned for being cheeky and even a little naughty, but Rooni here is quite the opposite! She is so sweet and gentle, which you can totally tell because of her cute outfit combo. Pick a feature fabric and team it with a matching stripe or polka dot, then pick out a contrasting color from your main print for her shoes and rose.

face

1 Using the templates for the basic body, cut out, stitch, and assemble Rooni's body and limbs, following the instructions on page 14. Cut two heads and four ears from brown felt. Cut two inner ears, one face, and both muzzle pieces from caramel-colored felt. Cut two eyes from black felt.

2 Lay the face panel onto one of the head pieces and hold it in place with glue or pins. Backstitch all around the edge, sewing through both layers.

3 Place the top muzzle piece on the lower muzzle, overlapping it by approximately ¼in (5mm) and gluing it in place. Backstitch through both layers in a line across the muzzle. In black thread, stitch two small lazy daisy stitches onto the top muzzle to represent nostrils.

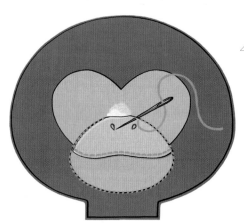

4 Place the muzzle on the face panel, lining up the bottom edges and pinning it in place. Whip stitch all around the edges, very lightly stuffing the muzzle before you finish stitching the whole way around, just to add a bit of definition to the face.

5 Using the photographs as a guide, sew the eyes in place with blanket stitch and embroider eyelashes using some free-form straight stitches. Finish the eyes by adding two highlights to each with white thread (page 12 has ideas and advice for embroidering lashes and highlights).

attaching the doll's head

Once you've finished Rooni's face and ears, follow the instructions on page 15 to attach her head to her body. Add a little color to Rooni's cheeks using the pastel or blusher (see page 13 for more about tinting felt).

head

1 Pin the front and the back of the head right sides together and backstitch all around the outer edge, leaving the neck area open (see page 15).

2 Turn the head right side out, push out the seams, and stuff it (page 15 has more advice on stuffing a doll).

ears

1 Place an inner ear onto an outer ear and hold it in place with glue or some pins. Whip stitch the layers together around the curved edge.

2 Place the stitched outer ear wrong sides together with a plain outer ear and whip stitch all around the curved edge, leaving the bottom edge open. Repeat to make a second ear.

3 Place an ear on either side of the head, positioning them so that the ends of the ear seam touch the head seam. Separate the front and back layers just a little so that the ear straddles the seam. Secure each ear with a few pins pushed through the base of the ear and down into the head. Ladder stitch all around the base of each ear.

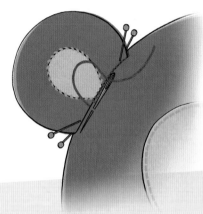

clothes and accessories

All the clothes patterns are on pages 130–134.

Rooni's ruffle-trimmed smock is made in bunny-print cotton fabric.

The Mary Jane shoes are made from lilac felt.

Rooni's rose is made from felt that matches her shoes.

Her shorts are made using the underwear pattern and striped cotton fabric.

Tip: Change the trim used for Rooni's top— try mini pom-pom trim, scalloped lace, crocheted lace, or fringing.

sofia the parrot

The scarlet macaw is a true reflection of just how wondrous Mother Nature is. It is a simply magnificent bird, and a riot of color. Sofia is quick and simple to put together, despite her detailed wings and eyes. She would look amazing in a jungle-themed room or displayed in a line with Stella the Penguin (see page 106) and Joni the Barn Owl (see page 42).

cutting out the doll

Cut out two bodies, one base, and four wings from red felt. Cut two eye patches and two beaks from white felt. Cut two lower beaks, one under beak, and two eyes from black felt. Cut two feather strips from each of red, yellow, green, and blue felt.

face

1 Glue one lower beak in place over one of the white beak pieces, matching the bottom edges perfectly. Whip stitch the pieces together along the top edge. Repeat with the second beak pieces.

2 Place the two beak pieces wrong sides together and whip stitch down the center using white thread. Stop sewing when you get to the black felt.

3 Add the under beak piece by whip stitching the two curved sides to the lower edges of the beak. Lightly stuff the beak, which will be added later after the body is put together.

4 Using the beak to help with placement (you can temporarily pin it to the head if that helps), use glue to hold the eyes patches in place. Sew around the edges with small whip stitches.

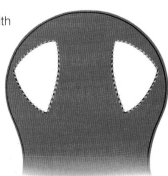

5 Using the photographs as a guide, sew the eyes in place with blanket stitch and embroider eyelashes using some free-form straight stitches. Finish the eyes by adding highlights with white thread (page 12 has ideas and advice for embroidering lashes and highlights).

6 Lightly sketch a spiral around each eye—as the spiral gets bigger the lines should run off the edges of the eye patches. These lines don't have to be perfectly parallel. Sew the spirals using red thread and running stitch.

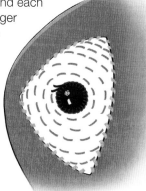

body

1 Pin the front and back body pieces right sides together and backstitch around the sides and the head, leaving the base open.

2 Turn the body right side out and stuff it. Stuff the head and body quite firmly, but leave the very bottom of the body only lightly filled for now; as you sew in the base you can add more stuffing to make it firm (page 15 has more advice on stuffing a doll).

3 Turn the parrot upside down and place the base over the opening at the bottom. Use ladder stitch to sew the base to the body all the way around. Add more toy stuffing as you go, but don't over-stuff or the base will become rounded and the parrot won't stand up straight.

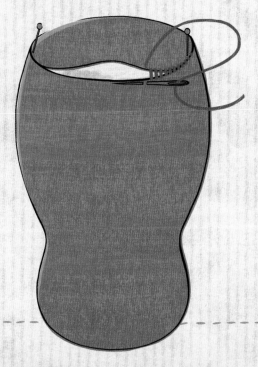

beak

1 Position the beak on the head and hold it in place with pins pushed through the beak and down into the head at a few different angles.

2 Ladder stitch all around the base of the beak, switching from white thread to black as the felt color changes.

wings

1 Place two red felt wings wrong sides together and whip stitch all around the edges. Repeat to make a second wing.

2 Begin layering the feathers from the tip of the wing upward. Start with one blue feather and use running stitch along the top to hold it in place, taking care to stitch through just one layer of the red wing.

Tip: Cut two feather strips from each wing color—red, yellow, green, and blue. Snip off one, two, three, or four feathers as you need them. Each wing will be a little different, and as it gets wider you can lay down a full strip, stitch along the top, then trim off any excess feathers.

3 Next, layer two or three blue feathers overlapping the first one slightly to cover the stitches. Sew them in place with running stitch along the top edge. Add a third layer of blue in the same way.

4 Continue in this way, adding two layers each of the green, yellow, and red feathers.

5 For the top layer of red feathers, do not use running stitch to hold them in place. Instead, secure them with the glue pen, then pin the wings to the body and whip stitch all around the top curve of the wing, making sure to sew through the red feathers, red wing, and the body.

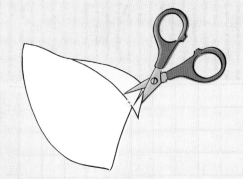

grass & desert

georgia the pig

This little pig Georgia is definitely giving some 90s vibes with this outfit. A ditsy print tea dress, denim jacket, black boots, and socks; I'm pretty sure I was dressed just like this circa 1995!

cutting out and making the doll's body

Using the templates for the basic body, cut out, sew, and assemble Georgia's body and limbs, following the instructions on page 14.

face

1 Cut two heads, four ears and both snout pieces from blush felt. Cut two eyes from black felt.

2 Beginning with Georgia's little snout, whip stitch one edge of the long strip all around the oval snout piece. Add two French knots for her nostrils. This snout will be sewn to the face later after stuffing the head.

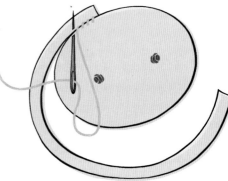

3 Lay the completed snout on the face to help with eye placement then, using the photographs as a guide, sew on the eyes using blanket stitch. Embroider some little eyelashes and add small white highlights with French knots (page 12 has ideas and advice for embroidering lashes and highlights).

4 Add a cute off-center smile by sketching a curved line with a fading fabric pen and embroidering it with backstitch.

ears

1 Place two ear pieces together and backstitch all around the edges, but leave the base open. Turn the ears the right way out and push out the seams. Repeat to make a second ear.

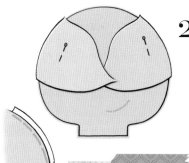

2 Pin the ears in place pointing inward over the face, as shown; the ends should extend past the edge of the head by about ½in (12mm). Then turn the head over and baste (tack) across the ends close to the edge of the head. Remove the pins.

Tip: The wide base of Georgia's ears help them to curve forward, but to further encourage the ears to curve, fold them down and pin them after she has been put together. Leave them like this whilst you make her clothes, then remove the pins and her ears will sit perfectly!

head

1 Pin the front and the back of the head right sides together and backstitch all around the outer edge, leaving the neck area open (see page 15).

2 Turn the head the right way out, push out the seams, and stuff it (page 15 has more advice on stuffing a doll).

3 Very lightly stuff the snout with just a pinch of stuffing, just enough to give it some body and to support the shape.

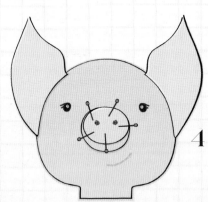

4 Secure the snout in place on the face using pins pushed straight down through the snout and into the head.

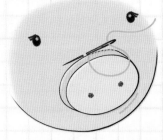

5 Ladder stitch all around the base of the snout. Remove the pins.

attaching the doll's head

Follow the instructions on page 15 to attach Georgia's head to her body. Add a little color to the cheeks using the pastel or blusher (turn to page 13 for more about tinting felt).

clothes and accessories

All the clothes patterns are on pages 130–134.

Georgia's ditsy print dress is trimmed with buttons.

Her denim jacket has little pockets and seam details for style.

Her underwear is made from thin cotton fabric.

Georgia's boots and socks are easy and quick to sew.

florence the cat

I don't have any cats at home, though I wish I did, but my neighbor has the most beautiful apricot-colored cat that I have ever seen! She often comes to visit my kitchen window to gracefully accept a treat or two. This pretty kitty is inspired by my neighborhood beauty queen, but you could easily adjust the colors and add more stripes, or even patches, to make a version of your own pet cat.

you will need

Basic doll templates on page 122

Cat head, face, stripe, and ear templates on page 125

Boat-neck dress pattern on page 130

Mary Jane shoe pattern on page 134

Underwear pattern on page 133

15 x 16in (38 x 40cm) of peach felt for body, arms, legs, head, and outer ears

2¾ x 2¾in (7 x 7cm) of white felt for inner ears and muzzle

2 x 3in (5 x 8cm) of ginger/orange felt for stripes

2 x 1¼in (5 x 3cm) of black felt for eyes

¾ x ¾in (2 x 2cm) of pink felt for nose

3 x 3in (8 x 8cm) of felt for shoes

2 x ¾in (5 x 2cm) of felt for Peter Pan dress collar

20 x 8¼in (50 x 21cm) of fine needlecord for dress (or cotton fabric can be used)

5½ x 5¼in (14 x 13cm) of cotton fabric for underwear

Basic sewing kit (see page 8)

Embroidery floss (threads) to match each felt color, dress fabric, and underwear

Glue pen

2 x snap fasteners

3 x ³⁄₁₆in (4mm) buttons

2 x flat-back pearls

Peachy-pink pastel or blusher

About 2oz (55g) of toy stuffing

face

1 Using the templates for the basic body, cut out, stitch, and assemble Florence's body and limbs, following the instructions on page 14. Cut two heads and four outer ears from peach felt. Cut two inner ears and one muzzle from white felt. Cut three forehead stripes and two eye stripes from ginger felt. Cut two eyes from black felt. Cut one nose from pink felt.

2 As there are lots of elements to the cat's face, it is a good idea to work out the placement of each piece before starting sewing. So arrange all the features on one of the head pieces and adjust them until you are happy with how everything looks. Then glue down the muzzle, the eyes, and the forehead stripes.

attaching the doll's head

Once you've finished Florence's face and ears, follow the instructions on page 15 to attach her head to her body. Add a little color to Florence's cheeks using the pastel or blusher (turn to page 13 for more about tinting felt).

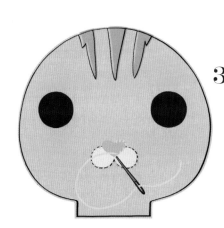

3 Whip stitch around the muzzle then the nose. Whip stitch around the three forehead stripes, keeping the stitches small. Blanket stitch around each eye.

4 Using the illustration as a guide, draw in the front line of the eye and the eyelashes using a fabric marker. Then backstitch over these lines with black floss (thread).

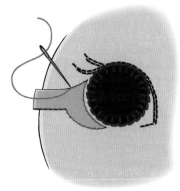

5 Now glue down the eye stripes at the outer edge of each eye. The ends of the stripes should extend past the head by about ¼in (6mm). Whip stitch around the edges of each stripe.

6 Add highlights to the eyes by drawing small crescent moon shapes on each eye. Outline the crescent shape with backstitch and white floss (thread), then fill the shape in with rows of backstitch. Finally add a French knot to each eye (page 12 has ideas and advice for embroidering lashes and highlights).

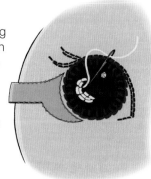

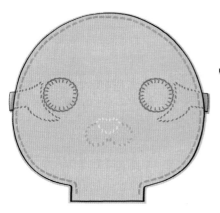

7 Pin the front and the back of the head right sides together and backstitch all around the outer edge, leaving the neck area open (see page 15).

8 Turn the head right side out, push out the seams, and stuff it (page 15 has more advice on stuffing a doll).

ears

1 Lay one white inner ear on one peach outer ear, aligning the bottom edges and centering the inner ear left to right. Backstitch around the inner ear, leaving the bottom edge open.

2 Place the stitched outer ear right sides together with a plain outer ear and backstitch around the outer edges, leaving the bottom edge open. Turn the ear right side out and press the seam out to get a smooth curve. Repeat to make a second ear.

3 Place an ear on either side of the head, positioning them so that the ends of the ear seam touch the head seam. Separate the front and back layers just a little so that the ear straddles the seam. Secure each ear with a few pins pushed through the base of the ear and down into the head. Ladder stitch all around the base of each ear.

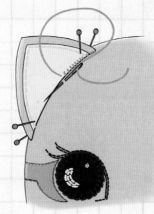

clothes and accessories

All the clothes patterns are on pages 130–134.

The dress's Peter Pan collar is made using the pattern for the front collar of the cape.

Her underwear is made from this cotton fabric.

Florence's Mary Jane shoes have little flat-back pearls added for embellishment.

you will need

Basic doll templates on page 122

Fennec fox head, face, ear, and flower templates on page 125

Sleeveless dress pattern on page 133

Mary Jane shoe pattern on page 134

Underwear pattern on page 133

Cape pattern on page 131

14½ x 16in (37 x 40cm) of cream or pale yellow felt for body, arms, legs, head, and ear backs

4½ x 6in (11 x 15cm) of white felt for ear fronts and muzzle

1½ x 1¼in (4 x 3cm) of black felt for eyes and nose

10¼ x 7in (26 x 18cm) of felt for cape

3 x 3in (8 x 8cm) of felt for shoes

3 x 3in (8 x 8cm) of felt for flower

20 x 8in (50 x 20cm) of cotton fabric for dress

5½ x 5¼in (14 x 13cm) of thin cotton fabric for underwear

Basic sewing kit (see page 8)

Embroidery floss (threads) to match each felt color, dress fabric, and underwear

Glue pen

1 x flat-back pearl

2 x snap fasteners

Peachy-pink pastel or blusher

About 2oz (55g) of toy stuffing

clara the fennec fox

Have you ever seen a real fennec fox? Oh my, they are so beautiful; with their wonderful ears and sweet little face, they are perfect! Clara's cape is simply embellished with a miniature flower brooch, but you could add all sorts of decoration—more flowers, buttons, or embroidery.

cutting out and making the doll's body

Using the templates for the basic body, cut out, stitch, and assemble Clara's body and limbs, following the instructions on page 14.

face

1 Cut two heads and two ears from cream felt. Cut both muzzle pieces and two ears from white felt. Cut two eyes and one nose from black felt.

2 Using the glue pen, stick the muzzle pieces together, with piece 1 on top of piece 2. Then place all the fennec fox's features onto one of the head pieces and adjust them until you are happy with the arrangement, then glue each piece in place.

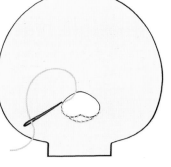

3 Whip stitch all around the muzzle.

4 Using the photographs as a guide, sew the eyes and nose in place with blanket stitch, Embroider eyelashes using some free-form straight stitches and finish the eyes by adding a few highlights with white floss (thread) (page 12 has ideas and advice for embroidering lashes and highlights).

5 Pin the front and the back of the head right sides together and backstitch all around the outer edge, leaving the neck area open (see page 15). Turn the head right side out, push out the seams, and stuff it (page 15 has more advice on stuffing a doll).

ears

1 Place one cream ear piece and one white ear right sides together and backstitch all around, leaving the base open.

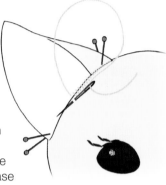

2 Turn the ear out the right way and gently push out the seams. Fold over the top corner of the ear by about ½–¾in (12mm–2cm) and make a few small straight stitches to hold the fold in place, making the stitches through the layer of white felt only.

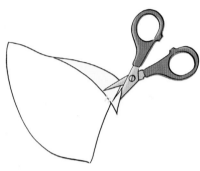

3 There will be a little triangle hanging below the base of the ear; simply trim this off flush with the ear base. Repeat to make a second ear, remembering to make it a mirror image of the first one.

4 Place an ear on either side of the head, positioning them so that the ends of the ear seam touch the head seam. Separate the front and back layers just a little so that the ear straddles the seam. Secure each ear with a few pins pushed through the base of the ear and down into the head. Ladder stitch all around the base of each ear.

Tip: You could always add some blusher to the inside of Clara's wonderful big ears. Tint them starting at the base and fading the color out as you work upward.

attaching the doll's head

Follow the instructions on page 15 to attach Clara's head to her body. Add a little color to the cheeks using the pastel or blusher (turn to page 13 for more about tinting felt).

clothes and accessories

All the clothes patterns are on pages 130–134.

Clara's dress is sewn from cotton fabric with a tiny floral print.

Her underwear is made from thin cotton fabric.

Clara's felt Mary Jane shoes are made in a color to complement her dress fabric.

Clara's cape is embellished with blanket stitch around the edges and a cute flower brooch. To make the brooch, simply cut out the flower template from felt and sew it to the cape with a few small stitches through the center. To finish it, glue a flat-back pearl over the top of the stitches.

maddie the elephant

Maddie's cute face is very simple and quick to put together, so she is a great project to start with if you are new to making and sewing. Her dress is made from two contrasting fabrics embellished with some simple glittery hearts. Play about with florals and stripes or polka dots to create an outfit for your own Maddie.

you will need

Basic doll templates on page 122

Elephant head, eye, trunk, and ear templates on page 125

Floaty dress pattern on page 131

Mary Jane shoe pattern on page 134

Underwear pattern on page 133

16¼ x 16¼in (41 x 41cm) of gray felt for body, arms, legs, head, trunk, and ears

¾ x ¾in (2 x 2cm) of black felt for eyes

¾ x ¾in (2 x 2cm) of pink felt for heart embellishment

7 x 4½in (18 x 11cm) of cotton fabric for dress bodice

20 x 5¼in (50 x 13cm) of cotton fabric for dress skirt

5½ x 5¼in (14 x 13cm) of cotton fabric for underwear

3 x 3in (8 x 8cm) of felt for shoes

¾ x ¾in (2 x 2cm) of gold glitter fabric for heart embellishments

Basic sewing kit (see page 8)

Embroidery floss (threads) to match each felt color, dress fabric, and underwear

Glue pen

2 x snap fasteners

Fabric glue

Peachy-pink pastel or blusher

About 2oz (55g) of toy stuffing

cutting out and making the doll's body

Using the templates for the basic body, cut out, stitch, and assemble Maddie's body and limbs, following the instructions on page 14.

attaching the doll's head

Once you've finished Maddie's face and ears, follow the instructions on page 15 to attach her head to her body. Add a little color to Maddie's cheeks using the pastel or blusher (turn to page 13 for more about tinting felt).

face

1 Cut two heads, four ears, and two trunks from gray felt. Cut two eyes from black felt.

2 Place the two trunk pieces wrong sides together and whip stitch all around, leaving the base open. Add the stuffing as you go because it may be difficult to reach the end of the trunk once it is completely sewn. So, once you have stitched the top of the trunk and about 2in (5cm) of the underside, start adding small pieces of stuffing. The long part should be quite firm and a little softer toward the base.

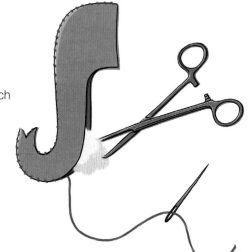

3 Center the trunk on the middle of the head to get the correct placement for the eyes. Make a mark where the trunk base will be and then set the trunk aside. Using the photographs as a guide, glue and then sew the eyes in place with blanket stitch and embroider eyelashes using some free-form straight stitches. Finish the eyes by adding a few highlights with white floss (thread) (page 12 has ideas and advice for embroidering lashes and highlights).

4 Pin the front and the back of the head right sides together and backstitch all around the outer edge, leaving the neck area open (see page 15). Turn the head right side out, push out the seams, and stuff it (page 15 has more advice on stuffing a doll).

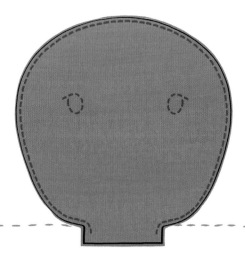

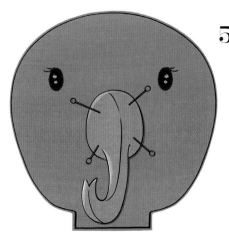

5 Place the trunk over the mark that you made earlier and hold it in place with pins pushed down through the trunk and into the head.

6 Ladder stitch all around the base of the trunk.

ears

1 Place two ears wrong sides together and whip stitch all around, leaving the base open. Do not cut the floss (thread). Repeat to make a second ear.

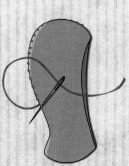

2 Place an ear on either side of the head, positioning them so that the ends of the ear seam touch the head seam. Separate the front and back layers just a little so that the ear straddles the seam. Secure the ear with a few pins pushed through the base of the ear and down into the head. Ladder stitch all around the base of each ear.

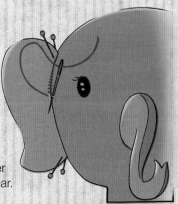

clothes and accessories

All the clothes patterns are on pages 130–134.

Maddie's dress is made using two contrasting fabrics—a stripe and a floral print. To make the simple heart embellishment, cut one heart from pink felt and another smaller one from gold glitter fabric. Glue both hearts to the bodice of the dress using fabric glue.

Maddie's underwear is made from this cotton fabric.

Her Mary Jane shoes are trimmed with tiny hearts cut from gold glitter and glued on.

bjorn
the sun bear

Bears are my favorite animals and I particularly love the sun bear. They are one of the smallest of the bear family, are known to be quite grumpy, and have a wonderful crescent-shaped marking on their chests. Folklore tells us that this crescent represents the rising sun, hence their name.

cutting out the doll

Cut out two bodies, four arms, four ears, and two foot soles from dark brown felt. Cut both muzzles and one crescent from caramel felt. Cut two eyes and one nose from black felt.

face and neck

1 Using the glue pen, stick the muzzle pieces together, with piece 2 on top of piece 1. Lay the muzzle on the bear's face, holding it in place with glue. Whip stitch the muzzle to the face, sewing right around it and along the line between the muzzle pieces.

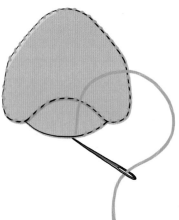

2 Glue the nose in place on the muzzle, then blanket stitch all around the edge of it.

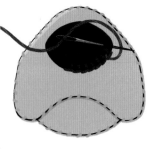

3 Using the photographs as a guide, sew the eyes in place with blanket stitch and adding highlights with white floss (thread) (page 12 has ideas and advice for embroidering lashes and highlights).

4 Glue the crescent shape to the lower half of the sun bear's neck and backstitch all around the outer edge.

body

1 Pin or baste (tack) the two body pieces right sides together.

2 Begin by sewing around the inner thigh area using backstitch. Note that there is much more of a seam allowance here than for the rest of the bear's body—this is to allow a nice curved seam when turned out the right way. So once you have sewn the seam, cut small notches in the seam allowance, close to the stitches but being careful not to snip them.

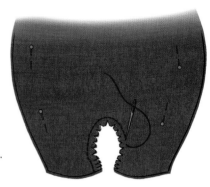

3 Sew all around the outer edge of the bear's body, leaving a turning gap of approximately 3in (8cm) in one of his sides. Leave the soles of the feet open.

Tip: Before filling the feet with toy stuffing, cut out two of the foot sole templates from sturdy (but not too thick) card. Trim a little extra off all around to make them just a bit smaller that the pattern piece and add them to the inside of the foot. This will help keep the shape of the foot and keep it flat.

4 Before turning the bear right side out, add the soles of his feet by laying the small ovals into the openings and either backstitching, whip stitching, or blanket stitching them in place all around.

5 Now turn the bear right side out and stuff it (page 15 has more advice on stuffing a doll). Close the gap with ladder stitch.

ears

1 Place two ear pieces right sides together ear and backstitch all around the curved edge, leaving the bottom edge open. Repeat to make a second ear.

2 Turn each ear right side out and press the seam out to get a smooth curve.

3 Place an ear on either side of the head, positioning them so that the ends of the ear seam touch the head seam. Separate the front and back layers just a little so that the ear straddles the seam. Secure each ear with a few pins pushed through the base of the ear and down into the head.

4 Ladder stitch all around the base of each ear.

arms

1 Place two arm pieces wrong sides together and starting about one-third of the way down the back edge, whip stitch all around. Stop about ½in (12mm) before the start of the sewing, but don't cut the floss (thread). Lightly stuff the arm, then continue the whip stitch to close the gap. Repeat to make a second arm.

2 Add the arms in much the same way as adding the doll arms (see page 15). Use a long doll needle and sew back and forth through the arms and the body until the arms feel secure.

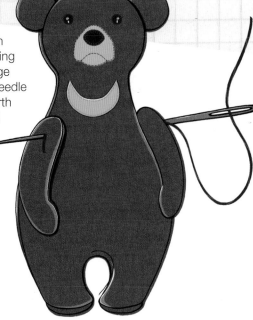

lana the pug

Pugs never fail to make me smile. They always look somewhat worried or even grumpy, which is ironic as a group of pugs is called a grumble! I just love their big round eyes, all the folds and wrinkles on their adorable faces, and the cute folded-down ears, which I can tell you are velvety soft in real life.

cutting out and making the doll's body

Using the templates for the basic body, cut out, stitch, and assemble Lana's body and limbs, following the instructions on page 14.

face

1 Cut two heads from light tan felt. Cut four ears and both muzzle pieces from brown felt. Cut two outer eyes from white felt. Cut two inner eyes and one nose from black felt.

2 Using the glue pen, stick the muzzle pieces together, with piece 1 on top of piece 2. Whip stitch the center peak, but don't cut the thread.

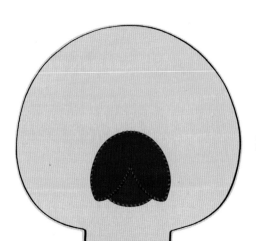

3 Glue the combined muzzle onto the pug's face and using the same thread, continue to whip stitch all around the edges.

attaching the doll's head

Once you've finished Lana's face and ears, follow the instructions on page 15 to attach her head to her body. Add a little color to Lana's cheeks using the pastel or blusher (turn to page 13 for more about tinting felt).

4 Sew the nose to the top of the muzzle using whip stitch. Sew on the whites of the eyes with whip stitch all around the edge. Then position the black eyes over the top, offsetting them a little so that the whites of the eyes show around the bottom half only, and sew them on with whip stitch. Finish the eyes by adding highlights with white thread (page 12 has ideas and advice for embroidering lashes and highlights).

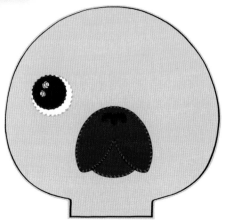

Tip: Play around with Lana's forehead wrinkles to get different facial expressions. Pull them closer together to make her look fierce or determined, or arch one side to make her look really quizzical.

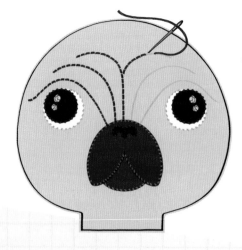

5 Using the photograph and illustration as a guide, sketch some forehead wrinkles onto the pug's face using the fabric pen. Backstitch each wrinkle using black thread.

head

1 Pin the front and the back of the head right sides together and backstitch all around the outer edge, leaving the neck area open (see page 15).

2 Turn the head right side out, push out the seams, and stuff it (page 15 has more advice on stuffing a doll).

ears

1 Place two pug ears together and whip stitch around the front and the short sides only, leaving the base of the ear open. Repeat for the other ear.

2 Pin each ear in place on the pug's head so that the base lies on the head seam and the ear folds inward and down on to the face.

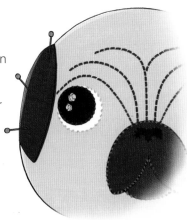

3 Starting at the top of the ear, ladder stitch along the outer layer of the base of the ear for about three-quarters of its length. For the lower quarter of the ear base, just whip stitch the two layers of the ear together without sewing the ear to the head. This helps the ear to sit correctly.

4 Gently fold the ear back and ladder stitch the inner layer of the ear to the head.

5 If need be you can add one or two stitches to the underside of the ears to help them sit in place. Take the stitches through the tan felt of the head and the under layer only of the ear, pull taut, and fasten off.

clothes and accessories

All the clothes patterns are on pages 130–134.

Lana's dress is made using a striped fabric for the bodice and small-scale clouds-and-raindrops print for the skirt.

Her boots are quick and easy to make from felt.

Lana's underwear is made from thin cotton fabric.

woodland creatures

aoife the doe

This wee deer is a sweet as can be in her pretty floral dress and lace bolero. Her name Aoife (say ee-fa) is an Irish name meaning "beautiful and radiant." Oisin on page 83 makes a perfect companion for her.

Oisin on page 83

you will need

Basic body templates on page 122

Deer head, face, ear, and spot templates on page 122

Sleeveless dress pattern on page 133

Mary Jane shoe pattern on page 134

Bolero pattern on page 131

Underwear pattern on page 133

14½ x 16¼in (37 x 41cm) of light brown felt for body, arms, legs, head, and ear backs

10¼ x 4½in (26 x 11cm) of white felt for face, ear fronts, and spots

2 x 2in (5 x 5cm) of black felt for eyes and nose

3 x 3in (8 x 8cm) of felt for shoes

20 x 8in (50 x 20cm) of cotton fabric for dress

5½ x 5½in (14 x 14cm) of lace for bolero

5½ x 5¼in (14 x 13cm) of cotton fabric for underwear

Basic sewing kit (see page 8)

Embroidery floss (threads) to match each felt color, dress, bolero, and underwear

Glue pen

4 x snap fasteners

Peachy-pink pastel or blusher

About 2oz (55g) of toy stuffing

cutting out and making the doll's body

Using the templates for the basic body, cut out, sew, and assemble Aoife's body and limbs, following the instructions on page 14.

face

1 Cut two heads and two ears from light brown felt. Cut one face, some spots, and two ears from white felt. Cut two eyes and one nose from black felt.

2 Lay the face panel onto one of the head pieces and hold it in place with glue or pins. Backstitch around the top, sewing through both layers. Do not sew around the cheeks or neck.

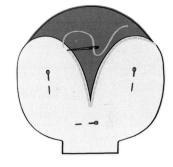

Tip: When I think of deer, my first thought is of their huge beautiful glassy eyes, so to get that real doe-eyed look, take your time stitching nice long lashes and big bold white highlights.

3 Using the photographs as a guide, sew on the eyes using a blanket stitch. Add some long lashes to each eye using free-form stitches, and add highlights using small moon-shaped pieces of white felt. Stitch over the highlights with a satin stitch or some straight stitches (page 12 has ideas and advice for embroidering lashes and highlights). Sew on the nose using blanket stitch and add a small white French knot to highlight it.

4 Now add Aoife's deer spots to the top of her head. Use as many or as few as you like, and you can trace around the templates or just cut out your own irregular circles and ovals. Blanket stitch them on in a random arrangement.

ears

1 Place one light brown ear and one white ear together and backstitch all around the edges, but leave the base open. Repeat to make a second ear, remembering to make it a mirror image of the first ear.

2 Turn the ears out the right way and push out the seams.

3 Gently tint the white of the ear with some peachy-pink pastel or blusher, starting at the bottom center and blending the color up and out (turn to page 13 for more about tinting felt).

4 Fold either side of the base of the ears into the center and secure with a few stitches (these won't be seen).

5 Lay the ears over the face with the brown side uppermost, positioning them as shown; the ends of the ears should extend past the edge of the head by about ½in (12mm). Pin the ears in place, then turn the head over and baste (tack) across the ends close to the edge of the head. Remove the pins.

head

1 Pin the front and the back of the head right sides together and backstitch all around the outer edge, leaving the neck area open (see page 15). Snip small notches in the ends of the ears extending beyond the head, then turn the head out the right way, push the seams out, and stuff it (page 15 has more advice on stuffing a doll).

attaching the doll's head

Follow the instructions on page 15 to attach Aoife's head to her body. Add a little color to the cheeks using the pastel or blusher.

clothes and accessories

All the clothes patterns are on pages 130–134.

Aoife's dress is made from cotton fabric with a small floral print.

Her little bolero is made from white lace.

Aoife's classic Mary-Jane shoes are made from felt.

For her underwear choose a thin cotton fabric.

oisin the stag

Oisin (say aww-sheen) looks so cool in his checked shirt and jeans. There are many checked cottons and fine denims out there to choose from, but you could always recycle an old shirt or pair of jeans that you already have and no longer use. Also, check out Aoife on page 80; they are the cutest pair!

you will need

Basic body templates on page 122

Deer head, face, ear, and antler templates on page 122

Shirt pattern on page 132

Jeans pattern on page 133

Boots pattern on page 134

14½ x 16¼in (37 x 41cm) of light brown felt for body, arms, legs, head, and ear backs

11 x 4½in (28 x 11cm) of white felt for face and ear fronts

2¾ x 3in (7 x 8cm) of dark brown felt for antlers

2 x 2in (5 x 5cm) of black felt for eyes and nose

8¾ x 8¾in (22 x 22cm) of cotton fabric for shirt

10 x 8¾in (25 x 22cm) of lightweight denim for jeans

4 x 3in (10 x 8cm) of felt for boots

Basic sewing kit (see page 8)

Embroidery floss (threads) to match each felt color, shirt, and jeans

Glue pen

5 x snap fasteners

4 x ³⁄₁₆in (4mm) buttons

Peachy-pink pastel or blusher

About 2oz (55g) of toy stuffing

face

1 Using the templates for the basic body, cut out, sew, and assemble Oisin's body and limbs, following the instructions on page 14. Cut two heads and two ears from light brown felt. Cut one face and two ears from white felt. Cut four antlers from dark brown felt. Cut two eyes and one nose from black felt.

2 Lay the face panel onto one of the head pieces and hold it in place with glue or pins. Backstitch around the top, sewing through both layers. Do not sew around the cheeks or neck.

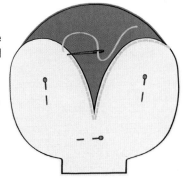

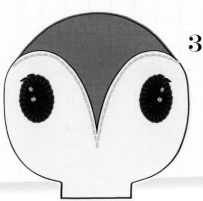

3 Using the photographs as a guide, sew on the eyes using a blanket stitch. Add some short lashes to each eye using free-form stitches, and add highlights using French knots in white floss (thread) (page 12 has ideas and advice for embroidering lashes and highlights). Sew on the nose using blanket stitch and add a small white French knot to highlight it.

ears

1 Place one light brown ear and one white ear together and backstitch all around the edges, but leave the base open. Repeat for the other ear, remembering to make it a mirror image of the first ear.

2 Turn the ears out the right way and push out the seams.

3 Gently tint the white of the ear with some peachy-pink pastel or blusher, starting at the bottom center and blending the color up and out (turn to page 13 for more about tinting felt).

4 Fold either side of the base of the ears into the center and secure with a few stitches (these won't be seen).

5 Lay the ears over the face with the brown side uppermost, positioning them as shown; the ends of the ears should extend past the edge of the head by about ½in (12mm). Pin the ears in place, then turn the head over and baste (tack) across the ends close to the edge of the head. Remove the pins.

antlers

1 Take two antler pieces and using a generous helping of glue pen, stick them together (the glue helps to add a little stiffness). Alternatively, you could stitch up the center of the paired antlers with backstitch.

2 Whip stitch all round the edges. Repeat to make a second antler.

3 Add the antlers in the same way as the ears, leaving approximately ¼in (6mm) extending past the edge of the head and basting (tacking) them in place. Tuck the antlers under the ears to help them lie flat as the two parts of the head are stitched together.

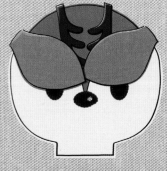

head

1 Pin the front and the back of the head right sides together and backstitch all around the outer edge, leaving the neck area open (see page 15). Snip small notches in the ends of the ears extending beyond the head, then turn the head out the right way, push the seams out, and stuff it (page 15 has more advice on stuffing a doll).

attaching the doll's head

Follow the instructions on page 15 to attach Oisin's head to his body. Add a little color to the cheeks using the pastel or blusher.

clothes and accessories

All the clothes patterns are on pages 130–134.

Choose a cotton fabric with a small check pattern to make Oisin's shirt.

His jeans are made from thin denim, or you could use needlecord for a different look.

Oisin's boots are very simple to make from felt.

Tip: If you are making Oisin and Aoife together as a couple, you can easily make one shorter than the other if you wish by trimming off ½in (12mm) or so from the tops of the legs before you sew the doll together.

you will need

Bear templates on page 123

Sweater pattern on page 134

20½ x 16¼in (52 x 41cm) of dark brown felt for body, foot soles, arms, eye patches, and outer ears

4 x 3in (10 x 8cm) of light brown felt for face

2¾ x 2in (7 x 5cm) of blush pink felt for inner ears

1½ x 2¾in (4 x 7cm) of white felt for muzzle

1½ x 1¼in (4 x 3cm) of black felt for eyes and nose

21¼ x 12in (54 x 30cm) of stretch knit fabric for the sweater

Basic sewing kit (see page 8)

Embroidery floss (thread) to match each felt color and the sweater fabric.

Glue pen

Peachy-pink pastel or blusher

About 4oz (110g) of toy stuffing

A small amount of card

ethan the spectacled bear

Bears in sweaters—what could be more adorable? Ethan's outfit is made from one of my favorite stretch knit fabrics, but you could always recycle an old knitted garment to make him a snazzy sweater.

cutting out and making the doll's body

Cut out two bodies, four outer ears, two eye patches, and two foot soles from dark brown felt. Cut two eyes and one nose from black felt. Cut two inner ears from blush felt. Cut one face panel from light brown felt and one of each muzzle from white felt.

face

1 Position the face panel on one of the heads and hold it in place with the glue pen or some pins. Backstitch all around the edge of the face panel. Then add the eye patches in the same way. Sew on the eyes using blanket stitch and add highlights using white floss (thread) and French knots (page 12 has ideas and advice for embroidering highlights).

2 The muzzle has two layers of felt to give some dimension to the mouth. Using the glue pen, stick the muzzle pieces together, with piece 2 on top of piece 1. Backstitch around the lips, sewing through both layers of felt. Don't cut the floss (thread).

3 Lay the muzzle in place on the face panel and backstitch all around the edge of it, sewing through all layers of felt. Sew the nose in place with a blanket stitch.

86 *woodland creatures*

ears

1 Glue or some pin an inner ear onto an outer ear, as shown. Backstitch the layers together all around, apart from across the bottom edge.

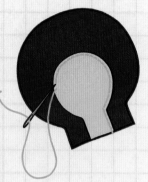

2 Place the stitched ear right sides together with a plain outer ear and backstitch all around, leaving the bottom edge open. Repeat to make a second ear. Turn the ears right side out and press out the seams to make neat shapes.

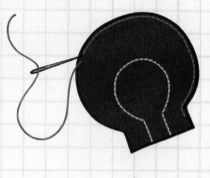

3 Position the ears pointing inward over the face, with the right side of the ears facing the right side of the face and the ends extending ½in (12mm) beyond the edge of the head. Pin the ears in place, then turn the bear over and use a small basting (tacking) stitch to secure the ears to the head. Remove the pins.

body

1 Pin or baste (tack) the two body pieces right sides together.

2 Begin by sewing around the inner thigh area using backstitch. Note that there is much more of a seam allowance here than for the rest of the bear body—this is to allow a nice curved seam when turned the right way out. So once you have sewn the seam, cut small notches in the seam allowance, close to the stitches but being careful not to snip them.

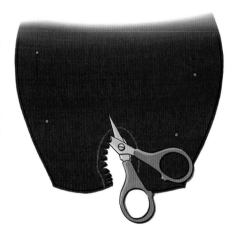

3 Sew all around the outer edge of the bear's body leaving a turning gap of approx. 3in (8cm) in one of his sides. Leave the soles of the feet open.

Tip: Before filling the feet with toy stuffing, cut out two of the foot sole templates from sturdy (but not too thick) card. Trim a little extra off all around to make them just a bit smaller that the pattern piece and add them to the inside of the foot. This will help keep the shape of the foot and keep it flat.

4 Before turning the bear right side out, add the soles of his feet by laying the small ovals into the openings and either backstitching, whip stitching, or blanket stitching them in place all around.

5 Now turn the bear right side out and stuff it (page 15 has more advice on stuffing a doll). Close the gap with ladder stitch. Add a little color to the cheeks using the pastel or blusher (turn to page 13 for more about tinting felt).

arms

1 Place two arm pieces right sides together and backstitch all around, leaving a gap of about ½in (12mm) for turning through. Repeat to make a second arm.

2 Turn the arms right side out and lightly fill them with toy stuffing. Close the gap with ladder stitch.

3 Add the arms in much the same way as adding the doll arms (see page 15). Use a long doll needle and sew back and forth through the arms and the body.

sweater

1 Cut two sweater body pieces, two sleeves, and one roll neck piece from the knit fabric.

2 Pin the front and the back of the sweater right sides together and backstitch across the shoulders; this should only be a few stitches across each shoulder.

3 Place one sleeve right sides together with the body of the sweater. Line up the edges of the sleeve head and the armhole a little at a time and backstitch the layers together as you ease in the sleeve. Repeat for the other sleeve.

4 Fold the sweater so that the front and the back are right sides together and the sleeves are halved lengthwise. Backstitch up each side to the underarm and then down the underside of the sleeve.

Tip: Knit fabric can be prone to fraying and unraveling, but finishing the raw edges of the bear's sweater seams with blanket stitch will combat this. So, after you have backstitched the shoulders, sides, and sleeves, go back and blanket stitch all the raw edges.

5 Turn the sweater right side out and try it on the bear, it will easily just pull over his head. Fold under and pin a small hem of approximately ¼in (6mm) (or more if you'd like the sweater to be shorter) around the bottom edge.

6 Remove the sweater from the bear and backstitch all around the hem.

7 With the wrong side edge of the roll neck collar just overlapping the wrong side edge of the sweater neckline, and beginning at the center back, simply backstitch the collar on all around the neck opening. As the wrong side of the collar is facing out, when the roll neck is folded or rolled down only the right side of the fabric will be seen.

8 When you get to the end, trim off any excess and backstitch the two short edges together on the wrong side. Then fold the collar down and put the sweater on the bear.

juniper the bunny

Did you know that rabbits are crepuscular, meaning that they are most active at dusk and dawn? This wee bunny, Juniper, is named after a dear young girl who absolutely loves animals, and who has the most wonderful name. Juniper the bunny is dressed in a lovely soft palette of blush pink, rust, and peach and you could easily make a gray or tan rabbit just by changing the main felt color.

you will need

Basic doll templates on page 122

Bunny head, ear, and eye templates on page 129

Sleeveless dress pattern on page 133

Blazer pattern on page 132

T-bar shoe pattern on page 134

Underwear pattern on page 133

17¼ x 16¼in (44 x 41cm) of white felt for body, arms, legs, head, and ears

2 x 1¼in (5 x 3cm) of black felt for eyes

20 x 8in (50 x 20cm) of cotton fabric for dress

16 x 12in (40 x 30cm) of cotton fabric for blazer

3 x 3in (8 x 8cm) of felt for shoes

5½ x 5¼in (14 x 13cm) of cotton fabric for underwear

Basic sewing kit (see page 8)

Embroidery floss (thread) to match each felt color, dress, and underwear

Glue pen

2 x snap fasteners

2 x flat-back pearls

3 x ³⁄₁₆in (4mm) buttons

Peachy-pink pastel or blusher

About 2oz (55g) of toy stuffing

cutting out and making the doll's body

Using the templates for the basic body, cut out, stitch, and assemble Juniper's body and limbs, following the instructions on page 14.

face

1 Cut two heads and four ears from white felt. Cut two eyes from black felt.

2 As there are lots of elements to the bunny's face, it is a good idea to work out the placement of each piece before starting sewing. So arrange all the features on one of the head pieces and adjust them until you are happy with how everything looks. Then glue the eyes in place.

3 Sketch the nose and mouth onto the lower half of the bunny head piece using a fabric pen. Draw a small but wide V-shape for the nose, add two curved lines extending down from the center of this V, and two tiny teeth in the middle. Backstitch these lines, slightly thickening the bottom of the nose with an extra layer of backstitches.

attaching the doll's head

Once you've finished Juniper's face and ears, follow the instructions on page 15 to attach her head to her body. Add a little color to Juniper's cheeks using the pastel or blusher (turn to page 13 for more about tinting felt).

4 Blanket stitch around each eye. Using backstitch, sew the curve at the front of the eye, then sew up over the top of the eye and out to make the lashes. First sew the basic lash shape, then go back and forth with straight stitches to thicken them at the base. Finish the eyes by adding French knot highlights with white thread (page 12 has ideas and advice for embroidering lashes and highlights).

head

1 Pin the front and the back of the head right sides together and backstitch all around the outer edge, leaving the neck area open (see page 15).

2 Turn the head right side out, push out the seams, and stuff it (page 15 has more advice on stuffing a doll).

ears

1 Place two ear pieces right sides together and backstitch the layers together around the curved edge, leaving the base of the ear open. Repeat to make a second ear.

2 Turn each ear right side out and press the seam out to get a smooth curve. Gently tint the white of the inner ear with some peachy-pink pastel or blusher, starting at the bottom center and blending the color up and out. Fold down and stitch the top corner of each ear base to the front layer of the ear only; just use a few small straight stitches quite close to the base. Remember to make the ears mirror images of one another.

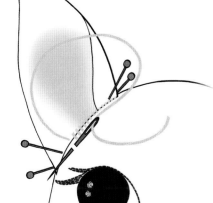

3 Place an ear on either side of the head, positioning them fairly high up and so that the ends of the ear seam touch the head seam. Separate the front and back layers just a little so that the ear straddles the seam. Secure each ear with a few pins pushed through the base of the ear and down into the head. Ladder stitch all around the base of each ear.

clothes and accessories

All the clothes patterns are on pages 130–134.

Juniper's sleeveless dress is made using a floral cotton fabric.

The neat blazer is made from cotton fabric and is trimmed with buttons.

Make the cute T-bar shoes from felt and attach a flat-back pearl to each one as a button.

Juniper's underwear is made from thin cotton fabric.

tara the unicorn

I wonder why we love unicorns so? It must be because of what they symbolize—magic, hope, goodness, love, and mystery. There are so many ways that you could personalize your own unicorn; change the hair color, make pastel rainbow hair, cut hair strands from glitter fabric to make streaks, add letters or motifs to the rump.

cutting out the doll

Cut out two bodies, two gussets, and four ears from white felt. Cut one horn from pale yellow felt. Cut two or three of each strand of the mane and the tail from lilac felt.

face

1 Using the photographs as a guide, sew one eye in place on each body with whip stitch, making sure to line them up and check the placement so that the eyes are level. Backstitch the curve in front of the eye, then add some eyelashes and white highlights (page 12 has ideas and advice for embroidering lashes and highlights).

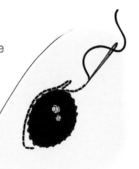

2 Embroider the nostrils using a French knot with a backstitch curl coming from it.

body

1 Place one of the gusset pieces on one of the body pieces and whip stitch all around the legs and undercarriage. Repeat to make the second half of the body, remembering to make it a mirror image of the first half.

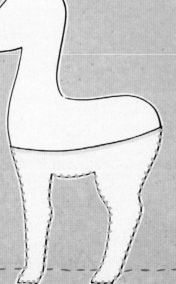

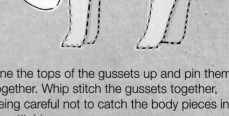

2 Line the tops of the gussets up and pin them together. Whip stitch the gussets together, being careful not to catch the body pieces in the stitching.

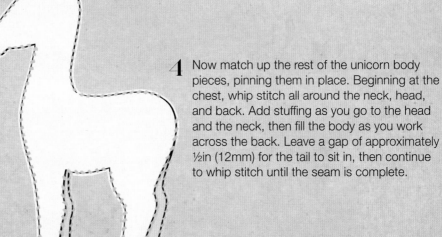

3 Stuff the legs, taking time to fill each little corner of the hooves (page 15 has more advice on stuffing a doll).

4 Now match up the rest of the unicorn body pieces, pinning them in place. Beginning at the chest, whip stitch all around the neck, head, and back. Add stuffing as you go to the head and the neck, then fill the body as you work across the back. Leave a gap of approximately ½in (12mm) for the tail to sit in, then continue to whip stitch until the seam is complete.

ears

1 Place two ear pieces right sides together and backstitch the layers together around the curved edge, leaving the base of the ear open. Repeat to make a second ear. Turn each ear right side out and press the seam out to get a smooth shape.

2 Using the photograph as a guide, place an ear on either side of the head. Secure each ear with a few pins pushed through the base of the ear and down into the head. Check the placement from all angles, then ladder stitch all around the base of each ear.

horn

1 Add some glue to one side of the horn piece and roll it into a cone. Add one or two pins to hold it in place until the glue dries. You may need to trim the base so that it is straight.

2 Bring the needle and thread up through the center of the horn and out at the top of the seam. Take a few small stitches to sew the seam down. Then wrap the thread around the horn once in a spiral line. Make another one or two stitches on the seam, then wrap the thread around again. Repeat this same process to the bottom of the horn.

3 Pin the horn in position centrally below the unicorn's ears, then ladder stitch all around the base.

mane

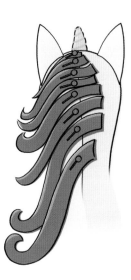

1 Beginning at the top of the head, start arranging the different strands of the mane so that they are shorter near the ears and longer as the mane goes down the neck. Pin the strands in place. You will need to trim some length from the top of some of the strands to make them shorter, but don't do this until you are happy with the placement.

Tip: There is no exact placement for the unicorn's mane or tail. Play around with the strands, trim them to make them shorter in places, change the direction of the waves; you could even add a few different colors, or many more strands.

2 Now trim the tops of the strands in line with the seam that runs down the neck.

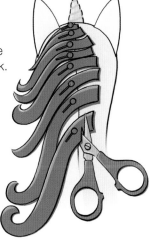

3 Starting at the bottom of the mane, whip stitch the ends of the strands to the neck, just covering the neck seam.

tail

1 Gather some strands of the tail together and play around until you are happy with how it looks. Then stitch back and forth through the base of the strands and wrap the thread around it to hold the strands securely together.

2 Insert the base of the pony tail into the gap left open earlier, adding a pin or two to hold it in place. Then ladder stitch the tail to the body all around the base. You can add extra whip stitches to the body seam above and below the tail if the gap is too loose.

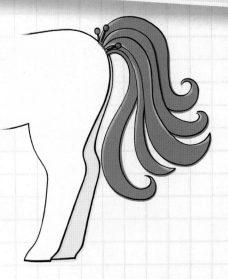

you will need

Basic body templates on page 122

Fox head, face, and ear templates on page 125

Sleeveless dress pattern on page 133

Boot pattern on page 134

Blazer pattern on page 132

Underwear pattern on page 133

Shoulder purse pattern on page 132

14½ x 16in (37 x 40cm) of rust-colored felt for body, arms, legs, ears, and head.

5¼ x 8in (13 x 20cm) of white felt for ears and face.

2 x 2in (5 x 5cm) of black felt for eyes and nose

7½ x 3in (19 x 8cm) of felt for purse

4 x 3in (10 x 8cm) of felt for boots

20 x 8in (50 x 20cm) of cotton fabric for dress

16 x 12in (40 x 30cm) of cotton fabric for blazer

5½ x 5¼in (14 x 13cm) of cotton fabric for underwear

Basic sewing kit (see page 8)

Embroidery floss (thread) to match each felt color, dress, underwear, and blazer

Glue pen

2 x snap fasteners

2 x ¾6in (4mm) buttons

1 x flat-back pearl

Peachy-pink pastel or blusher

About 2oz (55g) of toy stuffing

martha the fox

The beloved rusty-haired fox, I just adore their delicate pointy nosed faces and their beautiful coloring. My little fox, Martha, is quite the stylish young lady. Make her blazer from a fine cotton with a tiny stripe, pair it with a ditsy print dress, some navy ankle boots, and a slouchy purse and you have yourself one fashionable fox.

cutting out and making the doll's body

Using the templates for the basic body, cut out, sew, and assemble Martha's body and limbs, following the instructions on page 14.

face

1 Cut two heads and two outer ears from rust felt. Cut one face panel and two inner ears from white felt. Cut two eyes and one nose from black felt.

2 Lay the face panel onto one of the head pieces and hold it in place with glue or pins. Backstitch around the top, sewing through both layers. Do not sew around the cheeks or neck.

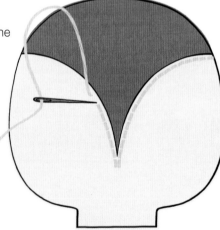

3 Using the photographs as a guide, sew on the eyes and the nose using blanket stitch. Embroider some eyelashes using free-form straight stitches and add some white highlights to the eyes (page 12 has ideas and advice for embroidering lashes and highlights).

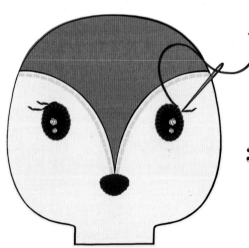

4 Pin the front and the back of the head right sides together and backstitch all around the outer edge, leaving the neck area open (see page 15).

5 Turn the fox head right side out, push out the seams, and stuff it. Fill it quite firmly around the seams and just a little more loosely around the neck opening (page 15 has more advice on stuffing a doll).

ears

1 Place one rust ear and one white ear together and backstitch all around the edges, but leave the base open. Turn the ears out the right way and push out the seams. Repeat to make a second ear.

2 Gently tint the white of the ear with some peachy-pink pastel or blusher, starting at the bottom center and blending the color up and out (turn to page 13 for more about tinting felt).

3 Place an ear on either side of the head, positioning them with the tips pointing upward and the ends of the ear seam touching the head seam. Separate the front and back layers just a little so that the ear straddles the seam. Secure each ear with a few pins pushed through the base of the ear and down into the head. Ladder stitch all around the base of each ear.

attaching the doll's head

Follow the instructions on page 15 to attach Martha's head to her body. Add a little color to the cheeks using the pastel or blusher.

clothes and accessories

All the clothes patterns are on pages 130–134.

Martha's cotton dress is made using a floral fabric.

Her jacket is a three-quarter-length-sleeve blazer in striped cotton.

Martha's boots are made from black felt.

The shoulder purse is trimmed with a single pearl.

Her underwear is made from thin cotton fabric.

ralph the wolf

The majestic and mysterious wolf is such a handsome creature. They are said to be the largest member of the dog family and while I have never met a real-life wolf, I have met a real-life St. Bernard dog, and he was huge! Ralph here—whose name, I'm told on good authority, means "Wolf Counsel"—is looking very casual-chic in his crisp cotton shirt and fine pinstripe shorts.

you will need

Basic doll templates on page 122

Wolf head, face, brow, eye, nose, inner ear, and outer ear templates on page 128

Shirt pattern on page 132

Shorts pattern on page 133

Boots pattern on page 134

16 x 16¼in (40 x 41cm) of marled gray felt for body, arms, legs, head, brow, and outer ears

2½ x 1½in (6 x 4cm) of black felt for eyes and nose

6 x 6½in (15 x 17cm) of white felt for face and inner ears

8¾ x 8¾in (22 x 22cm) of cotton fabric for shirt

10 x 5½in (25 x 14cm) of cotton fabric for shorts

4 x 3in (10 x 8cm) of felt for boots

Basic sewing kit (see page 8)

Embroidery floss (thread) to match each felt color, shirt, and shorts

Glue pen

3 x snap fasteners

4 x ³⁄₁₆in (4mm) buttons

About 2oz (55g) of toy stuffing

cutting out and making the doll's body

Using the templates for the basic body, cut out, stitch, and assemble Ralph's body and limbs, following the instructions on page 14.

face

1. Cut two heads, four outer ears, and one brow from gray felt. Cut two inner ears and one face from white felt. Cut two eyes and one nose from black felt.

2. Stitch the white wolf face shape on to one of the wolf heads. Pin or baste (tack) it in place and whip stitch only along the bottom, jagged edge of the white face. Remove the basting (tacking) stitches.

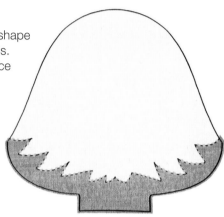

attaching the doll's head

Once you've finished Ralph's face and ears, follow the instructions on page 15 to attach his head to his body.

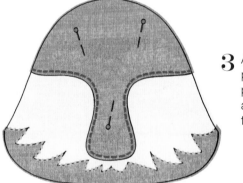

3. Add the wolf brow on top by pinning or basting (tacking) it in place, then backstitching all around the lower edge. Remove the basting (tacking) stitches.

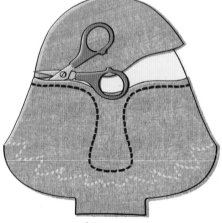

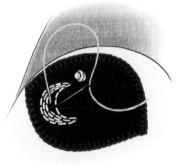

4. Your wolf's head now has three layers of felt at the top half, so carefully trim the bottom gray and middle white layer, leaving the brow layer in place. This will reduce bulk and make it much easier to sew the head together neatly.

5. Add the eyes and the nose by gluing them in place and blanket stitching around the edges. Embroider some crescent moon shapes onto the wolf's eyes for highlights. Outline the shape with backstitches, then fill them in with rows of backstitch. Add a French knot, too (page 12 has ideas and advice for embroidering lashes and highlights).

head

1 Pin the front and the back of the head right sides together and backstitch all around the outer edge, leaving the neck area open (see page 15).

2 Turn the head right side out, push out the seams, and stuff it (page 15 has more advice on stuffing a doll).

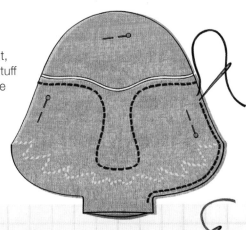

ears

1 Place an inner ear onto an outer ear and hold it in place with glue or some pins. Backstitch the layers together around the curved edge.

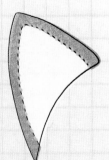

2 Place the stitched outer ear wrong sides together with a plain outer ear and whip stitch all around the curved edge, leaving the bottom edge open. Repeat to make a second ear.

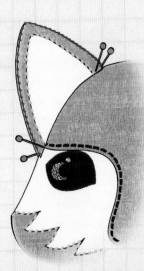

3 Place an ear on either side of the head, positioning them so that the ends of the ear seam touch the head seam. Separate the front and back layers just a little so that the ear straddles the seam. Secure each ear with a few pins pushed through the base of the ear and down into the head. Ladder stitch all around the base of each ear.

Tip: When a wolf meets its partner they stay together for life. Make Ralph his own soulmate by creating a second wolf and choosing any outfit from the clothing section that starts on page 130.

clothes and accessories

All the clothes patterns are on pages 130–134.

Ralph's cotton shirt is made from bird-print cotton fabric.

The knee-length shorts are made in fine candy-striped cotton.

Ralph's boots are a quick and simple make.

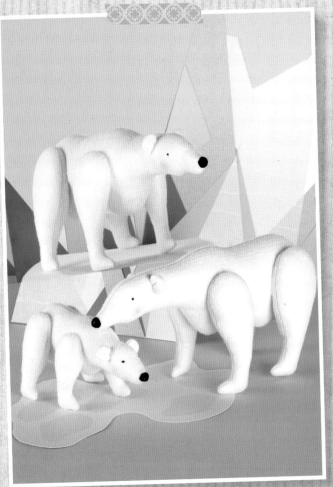

ice
& snow

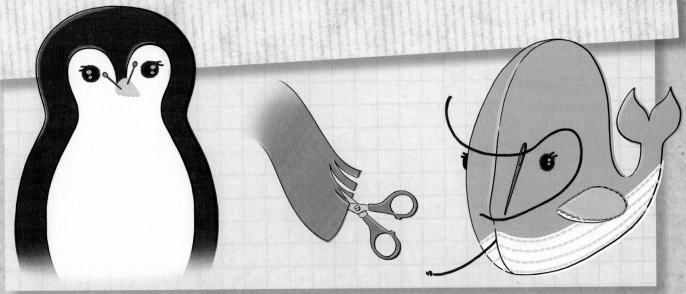

you will need

Penguin templates on page 124

20½ x 11½in (52 x 29cm) of dark gray felt for body and wings

6 x 9½in (15 x 24cm) of white felt for face/belly panel

1¼ x ¾in (3 x 2cm) of yellow or peach felt for beak

1½ x ¾in (4 x 2cm) of black felt for eyes

Approximately ½oz (15g) of mustard-yellow fingering weight (4-ply) yarn for the scarf

US1 (2.25mm) knitting needles

Basic sewing kit (see page 8)

Embroidery floss (thread) to match each felt color

Glue pen

Peachy-pink pastel or blusher

2 x ¼in (6mm) buttons to attach wings

About 4oz (110g) of toy stuffing

stella the penguin

Stella would make the perfect accessory for a little one's bedroom or play space. A quick and easy make, you will have her stitched in no time. Knit her scarf with just a small amount of yarn in a single color, or use lots of different colored scrap yarns to make her a stripy scarf!

cutting out the doll

Cut out two bodies, one base, and four wings from dark gray felt. Cut one face/belly from white felt. Cut two eyes from black felt. Cut two beaks from yellow felt.

body and face

1 Baste (tack) the face/belly piece onto one of the penguin body pieces, then backstitch all around the edge of the white panel. Remove the basting (tacking) stitches.

Tip: As the face/belly panel is quite big, I choose to secure it with basting (tacking) stitches instead of using a glue pen. It would require a lot of glue to hold it in place, but basting (tacking) stitches will hold it firmly, and they won't get in the way as pins sometimes can.

2 Using the photographs as a guide, sew the eyes in place with blanket stitch. Embroider eyelashes and add highlights with French knots in white floss (thread) (page 12 has ideas and advice for embroidering lashes and highlights).

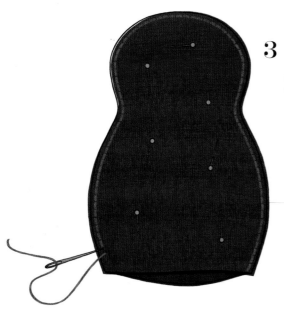

3 Pin the front and back body pieces right sides together and backstitch around the sides and the head, leaving the base open.

4 Turn the body right side out and stuff it. Stuff the head and body quite firmly, but leave the very bottom of the body only lightly filled for now; as you sew in the base you can add more stuffing to make it firm (page 15 has more advice on stuffing a doll).

5 Turn the penguin upside down and place the base over the opening at the bottom. Use ladder stitch to sew the base to the body all the way around. Add more toy filling as you go, but don't over-stuff or the base will become rounded and the penguin won't stand up straight.

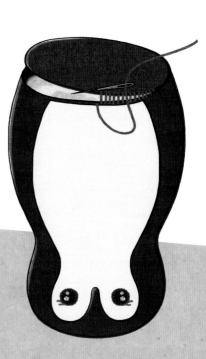

beak

1 Place the two beak pieces wrong sides together and whip stitch around the sides and tip of the beak; leave the base open and don't cut the floss (thread). Take just a pinch of stuffing and roll it between your fingers to make it smaller and sturdier, then add this to the inside of the beak, and snip off any excess.

2 Hold the beak in place on the face with two pins. Ladder stitch all around the base to sew it in place, removing the pins as you go.

3 Add a little color to the cheeks using the pastel or blusher (turn to page 13 for more about tinting felt).

wings

1 Place two wing pieces wrong sides together and whip stitch all around the edges, adding a very light padding of stuffing. You need just enough to give the wing a bit of body but not enough to change the shape of it. Repeat to make a second wing.

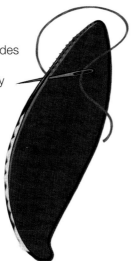

2 Add the wings in much the same way as adding the doll arms (see page 15). Use a long doll needle and sew back and forth through the arms and the body, adding buttons at the end for extra security.

seed (moss) stitch scarf

Cast on 11 stitches.
Every row: K1, p1 to the end of the row.
Rep this row for around 29½in (75cm).
Bind (cast) off.

Tip: If you aren't a knitter, either ask a knitting friend to whip up a scarf for you, or make a fabric one yourself from a strip of jersey or fleece fabric.

If you do knit, try casting on more or fewer stitches to make a thicker or thinner scarf, and play around with different weights of yarn and sizes of needles. Use scraps of yarn to make stripes. Design your very own mini scarf!

the polar bear family

Of all the animals in the world, polar bears are my ultimate favorite. This family of polars have become a dear tradition in my home; as soon as winter arrives they are proudly displayed in the window. At Christmas I add a bow of candy-cane striped ribbon around their necks, and I sometimes arrange them on snow blankets with tiny white twinkling fairy lights.

you will need

Polar bear body, leg, and ear templates on page 126

25½ x 13in (65 x 33cm) of white felt for papa bear

24 x 12¼in (61 x 31cm) of white felt for mama bear

16 x 8in (40 x 20cm) of white felt for baby bear

Basic sewing kit (see page 8)

Embroidery floss (threads) in white and black

Peachy-pink pastel or blusher

About 2oz (55g) of toy stuffing for each bear

cutting out the dolls

For each bear, cut out two bodies, four back legs, four front legs, and four ears from white felt.

Papa Bear, Mama Bear, and Baby Bear are all made using the same instructions. Where three measurements are given, they refer to the different-sized bears.

body

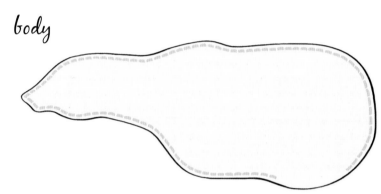

1 Pin or baste (tack) two body pieces right sides together. Begin backstitching them together in the back half of the undercarriage and sew all around, leaving a 1in/1½in/2in (2.5cm/3.75cm/5cm) gap for turning through. Turn the body right side out.

2 Pin or baste (tack) two matching leg pieces right sides together. Begin backstitching them together at the lower half of the back of the leg and sew all around, leaving a ½in/¾in/1in (12mm/2cm/2.5cm) gap for turning through. Turn the leg right side out. Make three more legs in the same way.

3 Begin stuffing the nose and head of the bear, making sure to fill each little curve (page 15 has more advice on stuffing a doll). Add more stuffing to fill out to the rest of the body so that the seams are nicely curved, but do not stuff the bear too firmly. Close the gap with ladder stitch.

4 Stuff each leg starting with the foot, taking care to fill the small curves. The paws and the lower legs should be filled quite firmly, while the top one-third of the leg should only be softly filled. Close the gap with ladder stitch.

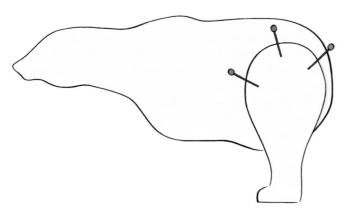

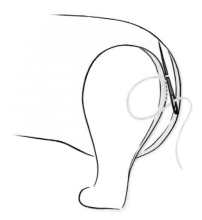

5 Attach the legs one at a time, starting with a back leg. Place it quite high on the body and secure it with pins pushed through the leg and into the body. (If you have long doll needles or extra-long pins, they will be useful here.)

6 Use ladder stitch to sew the leg in place: the stitches should go from the body to just behind the leg seam. Only stitch around the top one-third of each leg because ladder stitching too low could distort the body and legs.

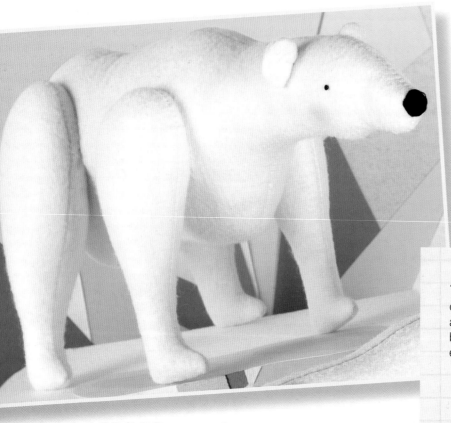

7 Repeat Steps 5–6 for the opposite back leg: check the leg placement from all angles to make sure they are even before stitching. Then attach both front legs in the same way, standing the bear on a flat surface and regularly checking the leg placement from all angles at every stage.

Tip: You could easily just change the color of your felt and make a brown or black bear family, or even one in every color!

ears

1 Place two ear pieces right sides together and backstitch the layers together around the curved edge, leaving the base of the ear open. Turn right side out and press the seam out to get a smooth curve.

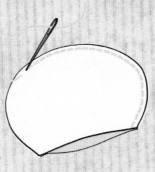

2 Pinch the front of each ear and secure the pinch with a few straight stitches (or a few ladder stitches).

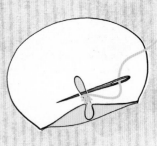

3 It is helpful to use a fabric marker to mark where the eyes will be in order to better place the ears. Use pins pushed through the ears and into the head to hold the ears in place. Ladder stitch all around the base of the ears. When sewing the back of the ears, make the ladder stitches deeper to help make the ears slope backwards a little.

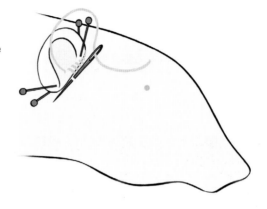

face

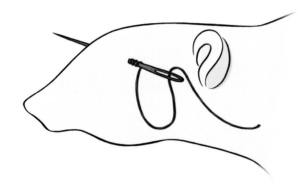

1 Add some black French knots for the eyes. Begin by bringing your needle up from under the chin, give a gentle tug to pop the knot to the inside and bring the needle out through the mark that you made for one eye. Make a French knot and bring the needle out on the opposite side of the head, where the other eye mark is. Finally bring the needle back out through the chin seam, close to, but not exactly, where you started.

2 The nose is embroidered using satin stitch. Begin by drawing the nose with the fabric pen, checking all angles to ensure it is evenly placed. Using two strands of embroidery floss (thread), bring the needle up from under the chin seam, hiding the knot just as before, and backstitch around the drawn outline. Then fill the entire shape with satin stitch, taking the ends of the stitches just over the backstitched line. Add a little color to the cheeks using the pastel or blusher (turn to page 13 for more about tinting felt).

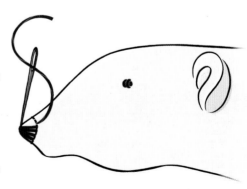

kai the whale & jade the starfish

These two are best friends, you hardly ever see one without the other. Kai swims much faster than Jade though, so sometimes she hitches a ride on his back! Both Kai and Jade are super quick and simple to make and are a great place to start if you've never made a softie before, or if you need a really quick handmade gift. Fun fact: a group of starfish is called a galaxy-isn't that lovely?

you will need

Whale

Whale body, belly, fin, and eye templates on page 127

10¼ x 12¾in (26 x 32cm) of light blue felt for body and fins

8 x 5¼in (20 x 13cm) of white felt for belly and fins

1½ x ¾in (4 x 2cm) of black felt for eyes

Basic sewing kit (see page 8)

Embroidery floss (thread) to match each felt color

Glue pen

About 2¼oz (60g) of toy stuffing

Starfish

Starfish body template on page 127

5½ x 9in (14 x 23cm) of pale yellow felt for body

Basic sewing kit (see page 8)

Embroidery floss (thread) in pale yellow and black

Strong fabric glue

15 x flat-back pearls—5 large, 5 medium, 5 small

About 4oz (110g) of toy stuffing

cutting out the dolls

Whale Cut out two bodies and two fins from light blue felt. Cut two bellies and two fins from white felt. Cut two eyes from black felt.

Starfish Cut two bodies from pale yellow felt.

Kai the whale

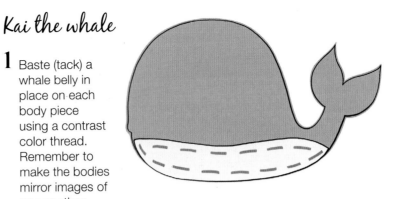

1 Baste (tack) a whale belly in place on each body piece using a contrast color thread. Remember to make the bodies mirror images of one another.

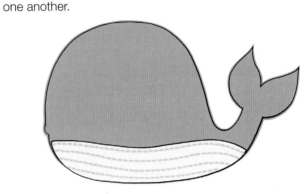

2 Backstitch three or four lines onto each whale belly; start at the top edge and follow the slightly waved shape of the belly. The lines do not have to be parallel, and in fact look good when slightly wobbly. Remove the basting (tacking) stitches.

3 Add an eye to each side of the whale using blanket stitch, checking that they are level. Embroider a few lashes and add two small highlights (page 12 has ideas and advice for embroidering lashes and highlights).

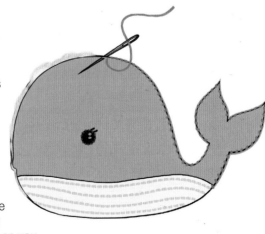

4 Place both halves of the whale body wrong sides together and whip stitch around the edges. Begin with light blue thread at the base of the tail, adding stuffing to the tail as you go. Continue around the body and head, changing to white thread when you get to the belly. As you close the gap, add stuffing to the body, filling it lightly (page 15 has more advice on stuffing a doll).

5 Place one blue and one white fin together and whip stitch all around with light blue thread, leaving the base open. Very lightly stuff the fin with just a pinch of stuffing. Repeat to make a second fin.

6 Secure the fin in place just above the belly, with pins pushed through the base and into the body, Whip stitch all around the base of the fin. Repeat for the opposite fin, checking the placement from all angles.

7 Add a little mouth by drawing it on first, then sewing it with backstitch. Take the needle and thread up through the seam a short distance below where the mouth will be, and tug gently to pull the knot inside the body. When you have embroidered the mouth, take the needle out through the same place.

Tip: Adding stuffing to the whale's tail as you go gives you better access to all the little points and curves, rather than waiting until the end.

Jade the starfish

1 Glue three pearls to each arm of one of the starfish bodies, starting with the largest closest to the center and finishing with the smallest at the point. Draw two dots and a tiny smile to make a face in the center of the body. Backstitch the mouth and add French knots for the eyes.

Tip: You could always replace the flat-back pearls with beads or small buttons, or if your Jade is intended for a little one, use some felt circles instead.

2 Place the front and the back of the starfish wrong sides together and whip stitch all around the edges. Start sewing in a corner, and each time you finish an arm of the starfish, very lightly stuff it (page 15 has more advice on stuffing a doll). Toward the end, add a little stuffing to the center.

arthur the polar bear

You may already gathered that the polar bear is my favorite of all the animals (and I do love them all). Many Northern cultures throughout history have given them different names, the White Sea Deer, The Rider of Icebergs, The Ever Wandering One, Isbjorn (the ice bear), or the Sailor of the Floe, but the name I like best is their scientific name Ursus Maritimus–The Sea Bear. So I thought it was only fitting that I should give my bear an apt name; Arthur is said to be derived from the old Celtic for "bear" and "king".

you will need

Bear body, foot sole, and arm templates on page 123

Polar bear muzzle, nose, eye, and ear templates on page 127

18½ x 16in (47 x 40cm) of white felt for body, arms, ears, and foot soles

2 x 2in (5 x 5cm) of black felt for eyes and nose

2½ x 3½in (6 x 9cm) of gray felt for muzzle

13 x 2½in (33 x 6cm) of fleece for scarf

Basic sewing kit (see page 8)

Embroidery floss (thread) to match each felt color and fleece

Glue pen

Peachy-pink pastel or blusher

About 4oz (110g) of toy stuffing

A small amount of card

face

1 Cut out two bodies, four arms, four ears, and two foot soles from white felt. Cut both muzzle pieces from gray felt. Cut two eyes and both nose pieces from black felt.

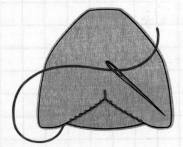

2 Using the glue pen, stick the muzzle pieces together, with piece 1 on top of piece 2. Whip stitch the center peak, but don't cut the thread.

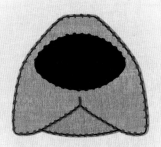

3 Glue the combined muzzle onto the polar bear's face and using the same thread, continue to whip stitch all around the edges. In the same way, layer the two nose pieces together and whip stitch around the nostrils. Without cutting the thread, position the nose on the muzzle and continue to whip stitch it in place all around the edges.

4 Using the photographs as a guide, sew the eyes in place with blanket stitch and embroider short eyelashes. Finish the eyes by adding a highlight with white thread (page 12 has ideas and advice for embroidering lashes and highlights).

body

1 Pin or baste (tack) the two body pieces right sides together.

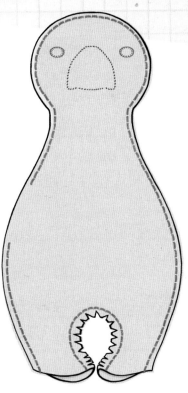

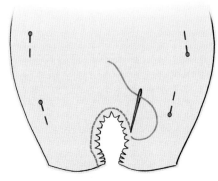

2 Begin by sewing around the inner thigh area using backstitch. Note that there is much more of a seam allowance here than for the rest of the bear's body — this is to allow a nice curved seam when turned out the right way. So once you have sewn the seam, cut small notches in the seam allowance, close to the stitches but being careful not to snip them.

3 Sew all around the outer edge of the bear's body leaving a turning gap of approx. 3in (8cm) in one of his sides. Leave the soles of the feet open.

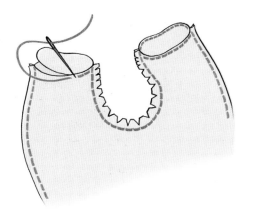

4 Before turning the bear right side out, add the soles of his feet by laying the small ovals into the openings and either backstitching, whip stitching, or blanket stitching them in place all around.

Tip: Before filling the feet with toy stuffing, cut out two of the foot sole templates from sturdy (but not too thick) card. Trim a little extra off all around to make them just a bit smaller that the pattern piece and add them to the inside of the foot. This will help keep the shape of the foot and keep it flat.

5 Now turn the bear right side out and stuff it (page 15 has more advice on stuffing a doll). Close the gap with ladder stitch. Add a little color to the cheeks using the pastel or blusher (turn to page 13 for more about tinting felt).

ears

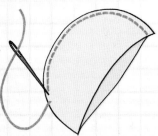

1 Place two ear pieces right sides together ear and backstitch all around the curved edge, leaving the bottom edge open. Repeat to make a second ear.

2 Turn each ear right side out and press the seam out to get a smooth curve.

3 Place an ear on either side of the head, positioning them so that the ends of the ear seam touch the head seam. Separate the front and back layers just a little so that the ear straddles the seam. Secure each ear with a few pins pushed through the base of the ear and down into the head.

4 Ladder stitch all around the base of each ear.

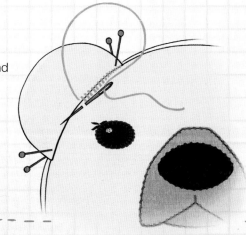

arms

1 Place two arm pieces wrong sides together and starting about one-third of the way down the back edge, whip stitch all around. Stop about ½in (12mm) before the start of the sewing, but don't cut the floss (thread). Lightly stuff the arm, then continue the whip stitch to close the gap. Repeat to make a second arm.

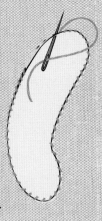

2 Add the arms in much the same way as adding the doll arms (see page 15). Use a long doll needle and sew back and forth through the arms and the body until the arms feel secure.

scarf

1 Snip into each end of the strip of fleecy fabric, making cuts about ¾in (2cm) long to make fringes.

2 This step is optional, but it is a good idea to add a few stitches where the scarf crosses over to keep it in place. Use a matching thread and make a few ladder stitches that go from the wrong side of the top layer and the right side of the bottom layer.

Tip: As with all the outfit and accessories in the book, you can easily adapt Arthur's scarf. Make it longer, shorter, wider, skinnier, use felt, knit it, crochet it, add a motif—the possibilities are endless! Ethan the bear's sweater (see page 90) will fit Arthur, as will Stella the penguin's knitted scarf (see page 109).

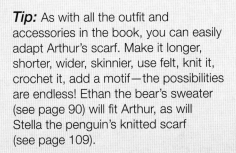

arthur the polar bear **121**

templates

All the templates in this section are printed at 50% of their actual size. They will need to be enlarged by 200% using a photocopier. Many items, such as bodices and skirts, have two back or two front pieces (or a left and a right piece). In these cases only one template is provided as the left and right pieces are exactly the same. All you need to do is cut two pieces, remembering to flip the template over if your fabric has a right and wrong side. See page 9 for more tips on using templates.

basic body

back

leg

arm

front

oisin stag and aoife doe p80

ear

spots

face panel

eye

nose

head

antler

georgia pig p58

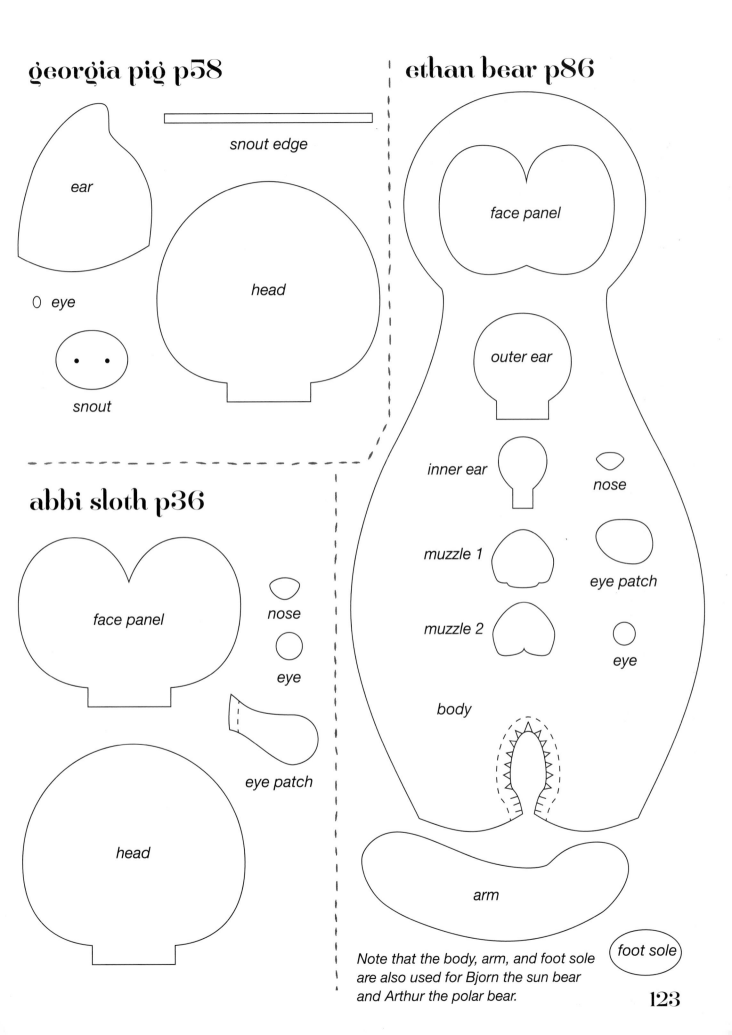

ear

snout edge

O eye

snout

head

ethan bear p86

face panel

outer ear

inner ear

nose

muzzle 1

eye patch

muzzle 2

eye

body

arm

foot sole

abbi sloth p36

face panel

nose

eye

eye patch

head

Note that the body, arm, and foot sole are also used for Bjorn the sun bear and Arthur the polar bear.

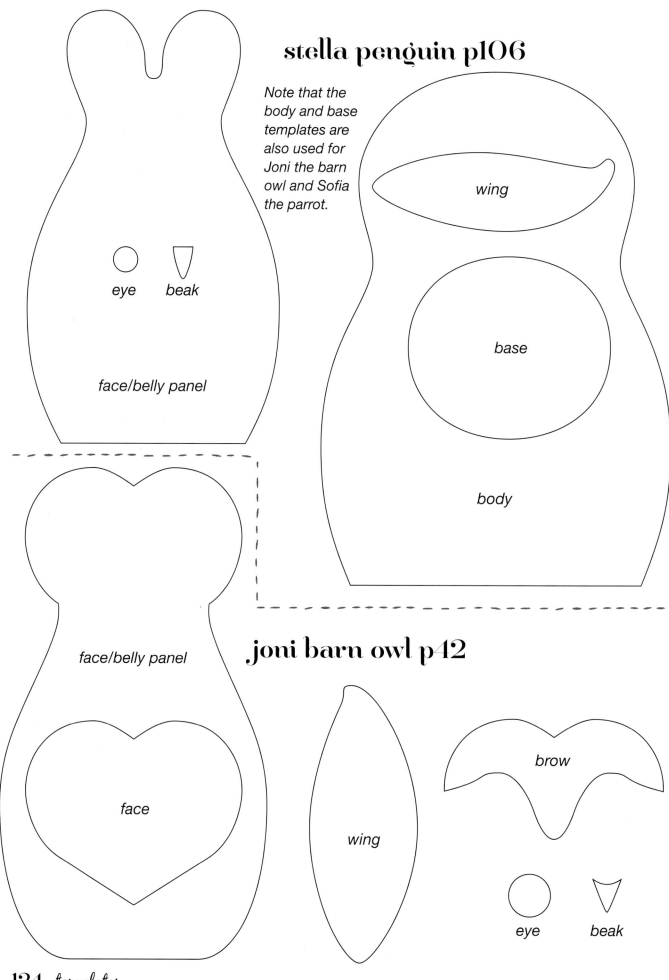

stella penguin p106

Note that the body and base templates are also used for Joni the barn owl and Sofia the parrot.

eye   beak

face/belly panel

wing

base

body

joni barn owl p42

face/belly panel

face

wing

brow

eye   beak

martha fox p98

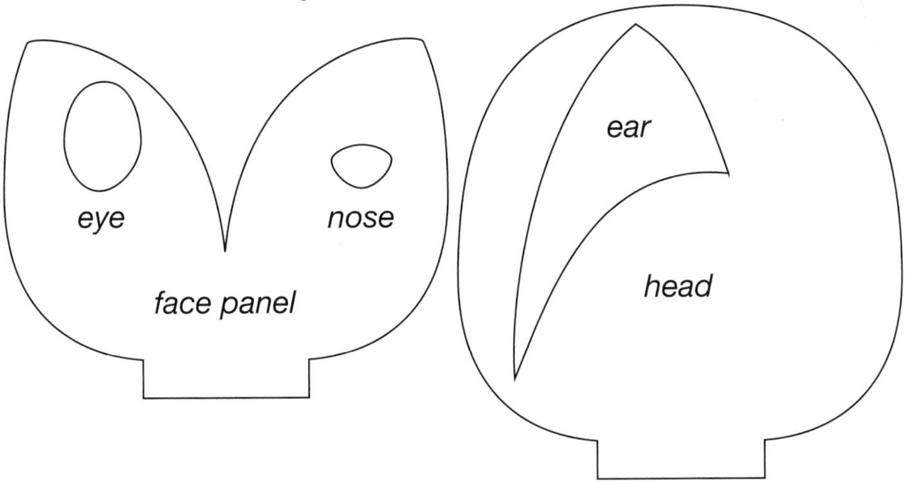

eye

nose

face panel

ear

head

pearl koala p30

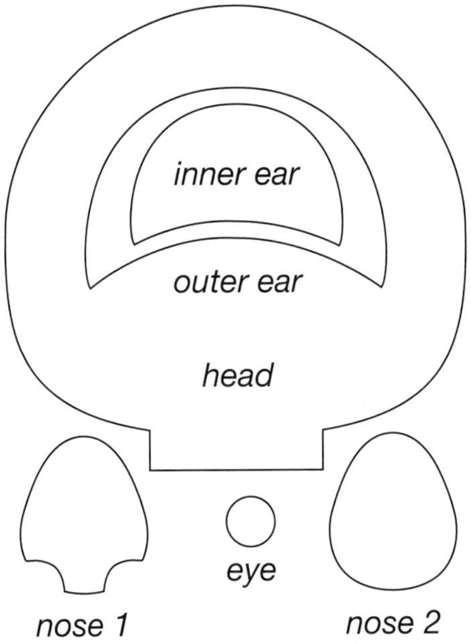

inner ear

outer ear

head

nose 1

eye

nose 2

florence cat p60

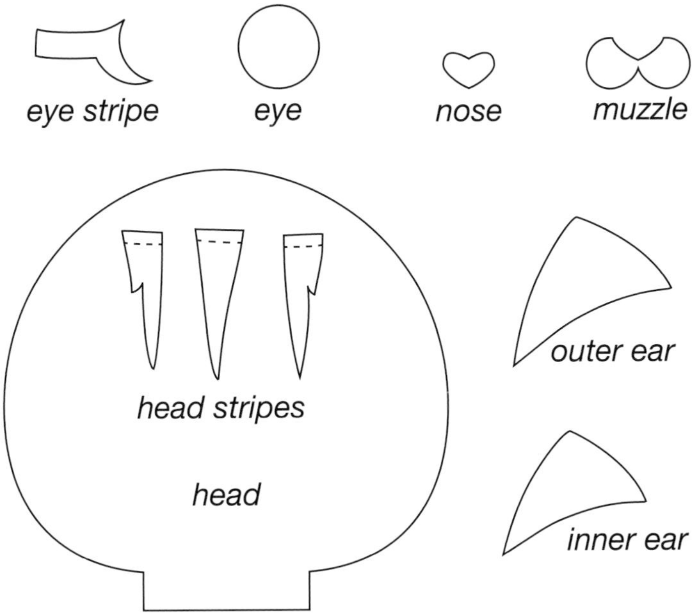

eye stripe

eye

nose

muzzle

head stripes

head

outer ear

inner ear

maddie elephant p66

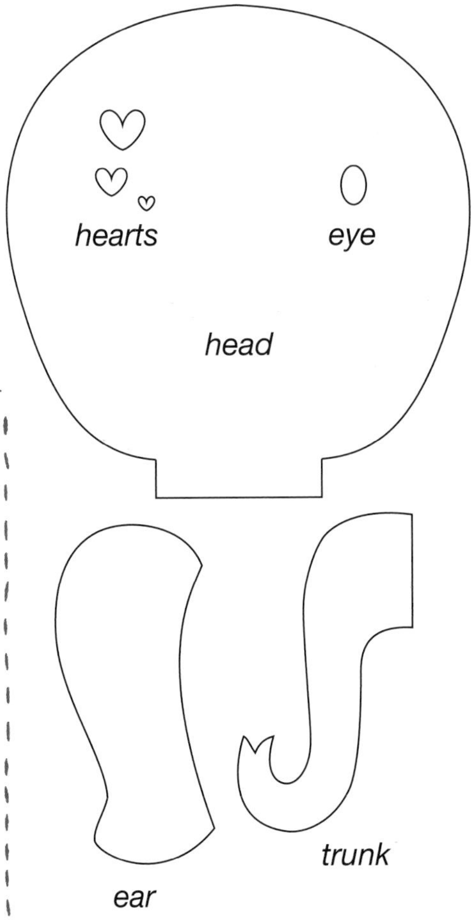

hearts

eye

head

clara fennec fox p64

muzzle 1

muzzle 2

eye

nose

flower

ear

head

ear

trunk

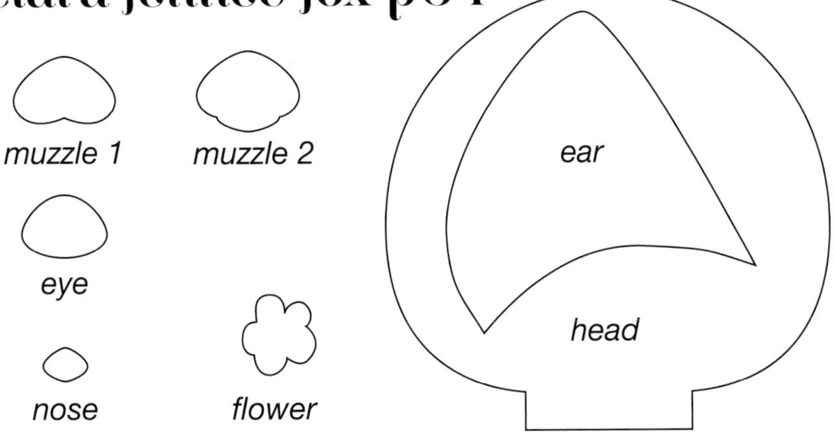

polar bear family p110

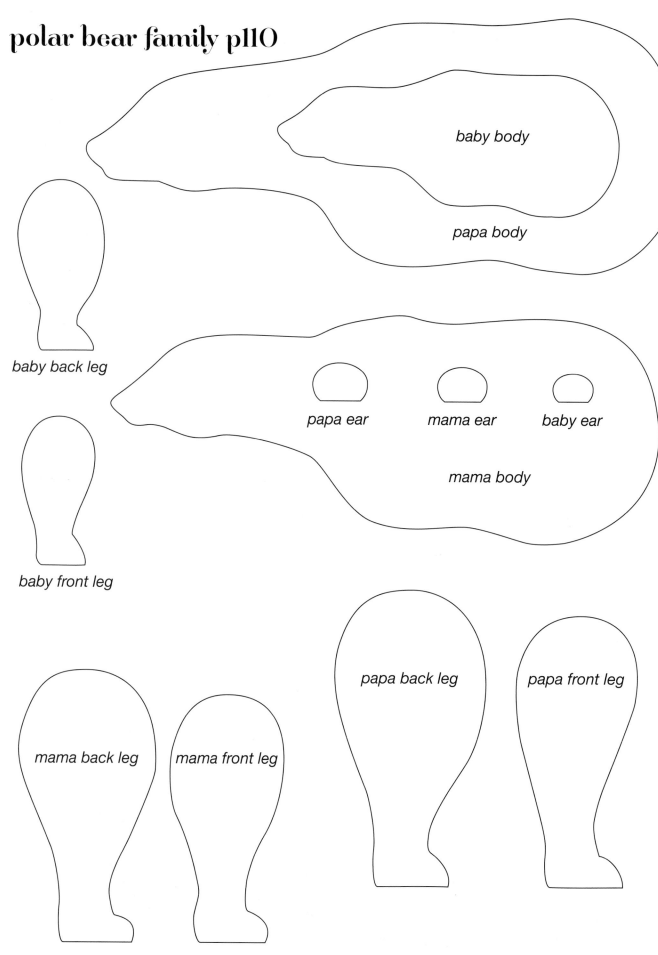

baby body

papa body

baby back leg

papa ear

mama ear

baby ear

mama body

baby front leg

papa back leg

papa front leg

mama back leg

mama front leg

jenny panda p46

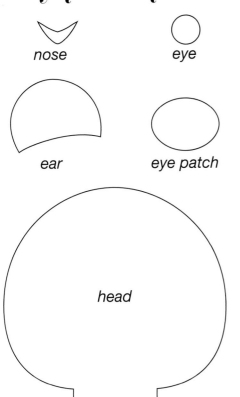

nose

eye

ear

eye patch

head

arthur polar bear p118

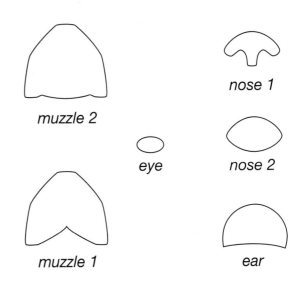

muzzle 2

nose 1

eye

nose 2

muzzle 1

ear

kai whale & jade starfish p114

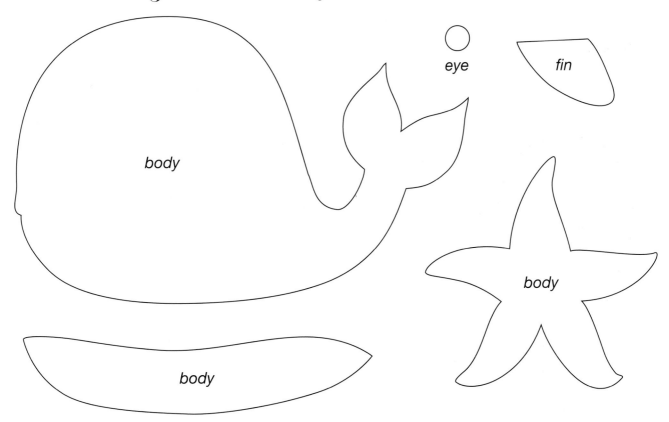

body

eye

fin

body

body

ralph wolf p101

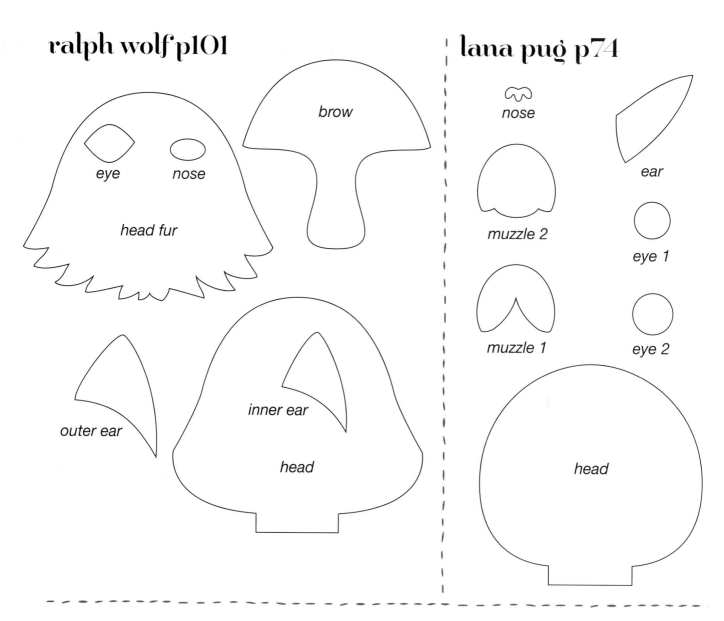

eye

nose

head fur

brow

outer ear

inner ear

head

lana pug p74

nose

muzzle 2

muzzle 1

ear

eye 1

eye 2

head

rooni monkey p49

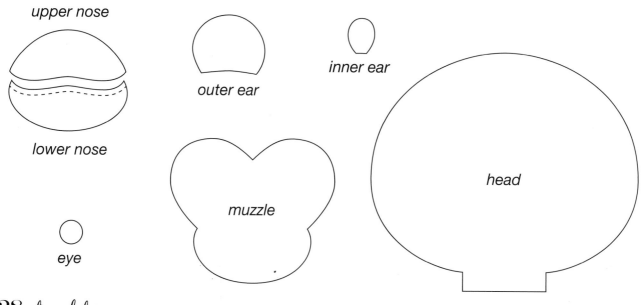

upper nose

lower nose

eye

outer ear

inner ear

muzzle

head

juniper bunny p91

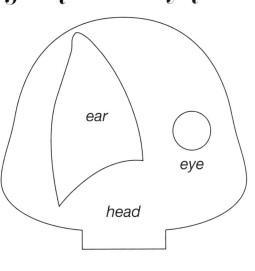

ear

eye

head

sophia parrot p52

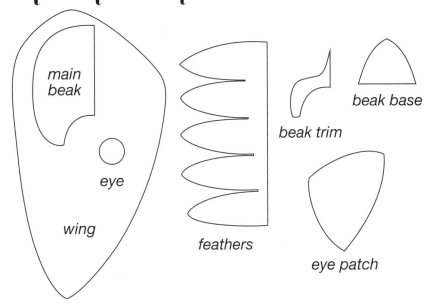

main beak

eye

wing

beak trim

beak base

feathers

eye patch

tara unicorn p94

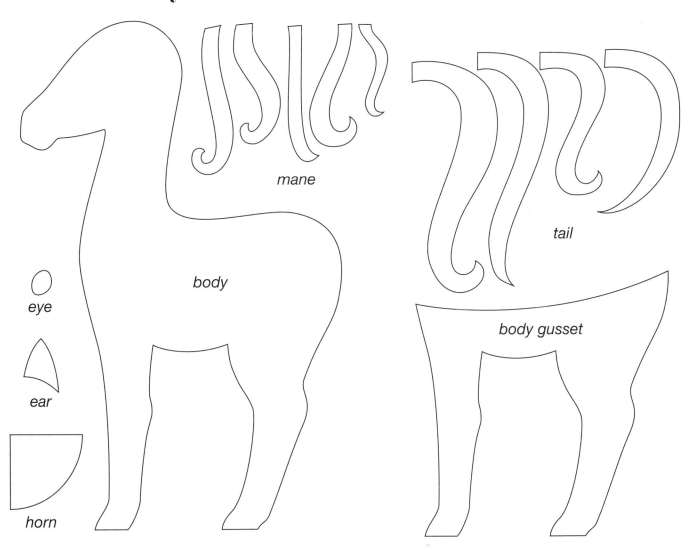

mane

tail

eye

body

body gusset

ear

horn

stevie raccoon p39

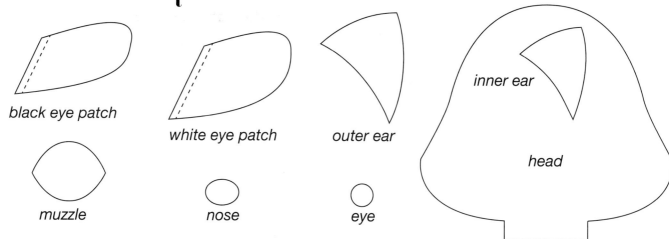

black eye patch

white eye patch

outer ear

inner ear

head

muzzle

nose

eye

bjorn sun bear p70

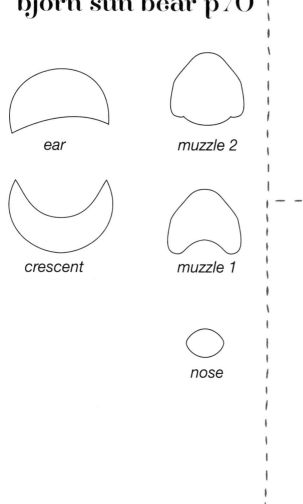

ear

muzzle 2

crescent

muzzle 1

nose

boat-neck dress

sewing instructions on p17

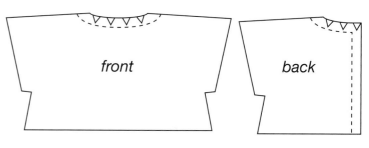

front

back

alfie red panda p33

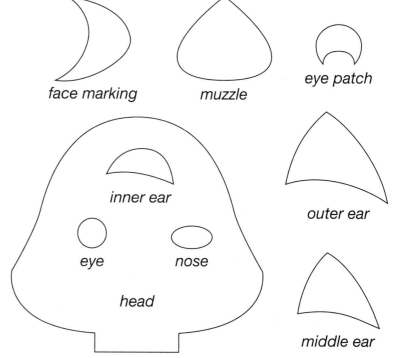

face marking

muzzle

eye patch

inner ear

outer ear

eye

nose

head

middle ear

cape
sewing instructions on p21

back

front

front collar

back collar

floaty-sleeve dress
sewing instructions on p18

sleeve

denim jacket
sewing instructions on p24

front

back

sleeve

pocket

faux seam

collar

bolero
instructions on p22

back

front

rose
sewing instructions on p25

shirt

sewing instructions on p20

sleeve

back

front

collar

stole

sewing instructions on p22

blazer

sewing instructions on p22

front

sleeve

shoulder purse

sewing instructions on p27

front

back

strap

pocket

back

clutch purse

sewing instructions on p26

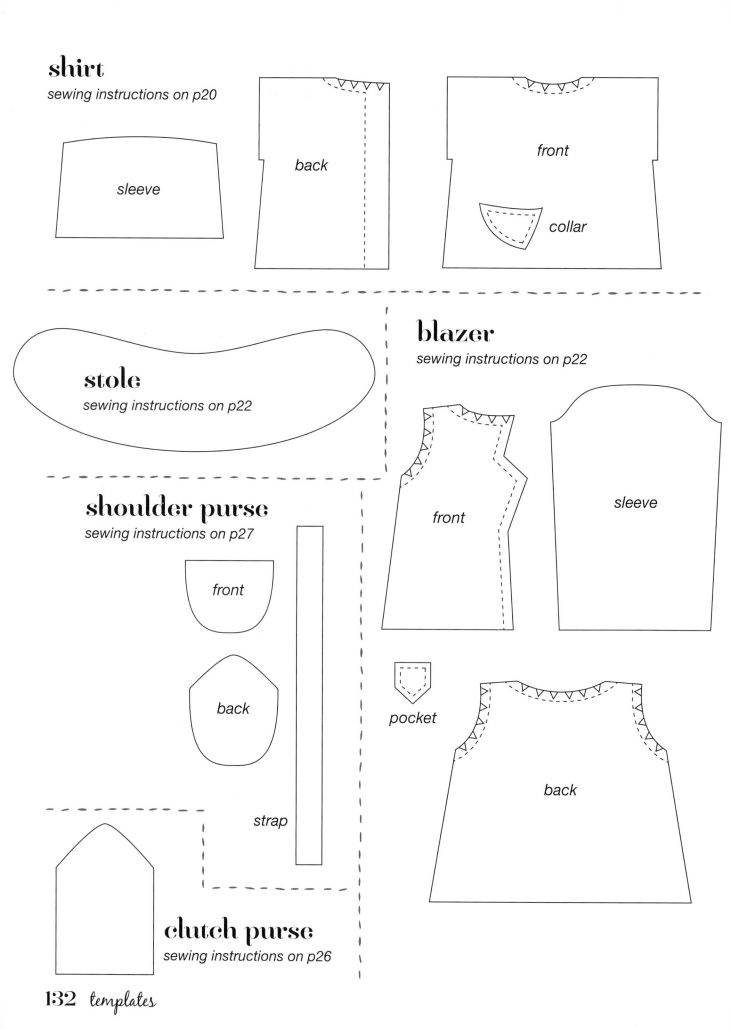

underwear
sewing instructions on p26

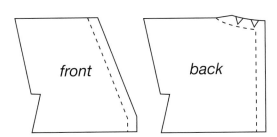

front and back

smock top
sewing instructions on p21

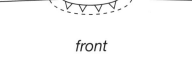

back

front

sleeveless dress
sewing instructions on p16

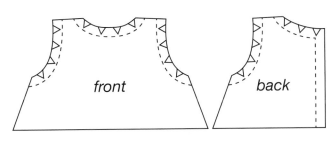

front

back

jeans and shorts
sewing instructions on p19

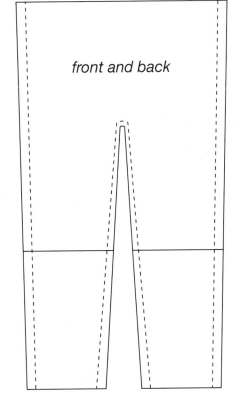

front and back

v-neck dress
sewing instructions on p18

front

back

shoes

sewing instructions on p27

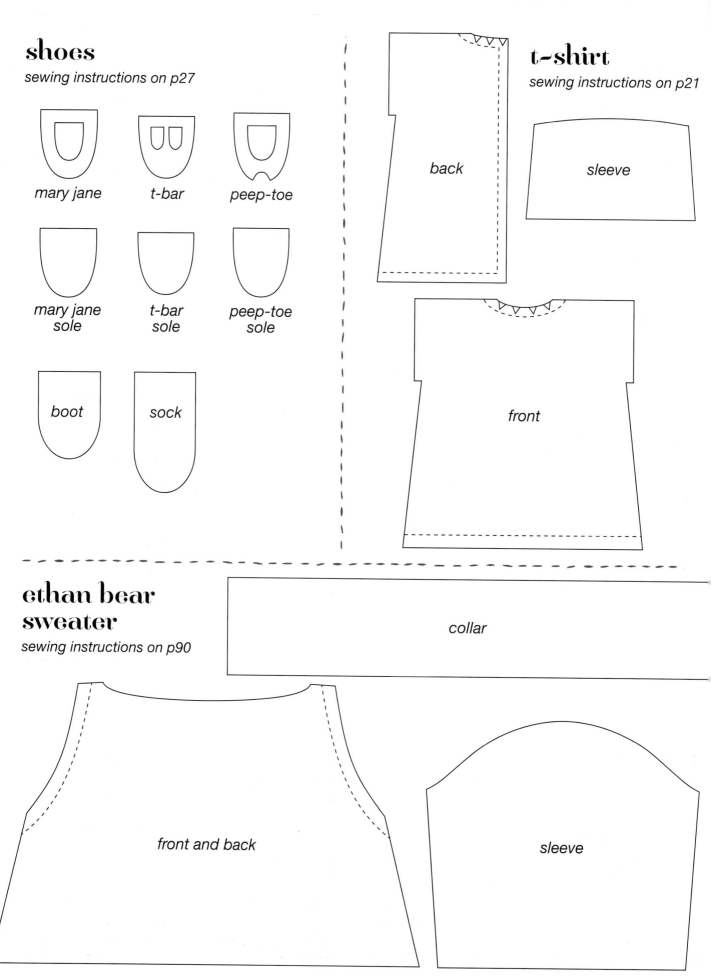

mary jane

t-bar

peep-toe

*mary jane
sole*

*t-bar
sole*

*peep-toe
sole*

boot

sock

t-shirt

sewing instructions on p21

back

sleeve

front

ethan bear
sweater

sewing instructions on p90

collar

front and back

sleeve